AUTUMN WINTER 2004
WWW.PAULSMITH.CO.UK

It is wise to adopt the pace of nature, her secret is consistency and patience.

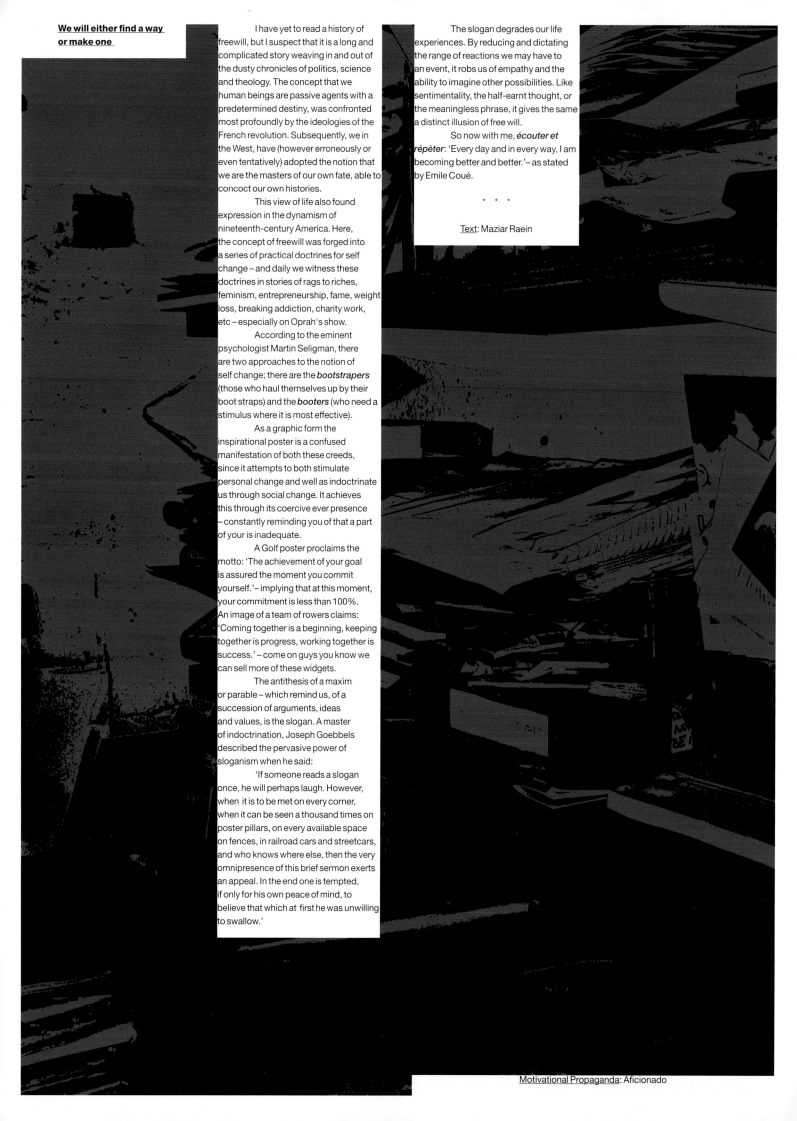

I have yet to read a history of freewill, but I suspect that it is a long and complicated story weaving in and out of the dusty chronicles of politics, science and theology. The concept that we human beings are passive agents with a predetermined destiny, was confronted most profoundly by the ideologies of the French revolution. Subsequently, we in the West, have (however erroneously or even tentatively) adopted the notion that we are the masters of our own fate, able to concoct our own histories.

This view of life also found expression in the dynamism of nineteenth-century America. Here, the concept of freewill was forged into a series of practical doctrines for self change – and daily we witness these doctrines in stories of rags to riches, feminism, entrepreneurship, fame, weight loss, breaking addiction, charity work, etc – especially on Oprah's show.

According to the eminent psychologist Martin Seligman, there are two approaches to the notion of self change; there are the *bootstrapers* (those who haul themselves up by their boot straps) and the *booters* (who need a stimulus where it is most effective).

As a graphic form the inspirational poster is a confused manifestation of both these creeds, since it attempts to both stimulate personal change and well as indoctrinate us through social change. It achieves this through its coercive ever presence – constantly reminding you of that a part of your is inadequate.

A Golf poster proclaims the motto: 'The achievement of your goal is assured the moment you commit yourself.'– implying that at this moment, your commitment is less than 100%. An image of a team of rowers claims: 'Coming together is a beginning, keeping together is progress, working together is success.' – come on guys you know we can sell more of these widgets.

The antithesis of a maxim or parable – which remind us, of a succession of arguments, ideas and values, is the slogan. A master of indoctrination, Joseph Goebbels described the pervasive power of sloganism when he said:

'If someone reads a slogan once, he will perhaps laugh. However, when it is to be met on every corner, when it can be seen a thousand times on poster pillars, on every available space on fences, in railroad cars and streetcars, and who knows where else, then the very omnipresence of this brief sermon exerts an appeal. In the end one is tempted, if only for his own peace of mind, to believe that which at first he was unwilling to swallow.'

The slogan degrades our life experiences. By reducing and dictating the range of reactions we may have to an event, it robs us of empathy and the ability to imagine other possibilities. Like sentimentality, the half-earnt thought, or the meaningless phrase, it gives the same a distinct illusion of free will.

So now with me, *écouter et répèter*: 'Every day and in every way, I am becoming better and better.'– as stated by Emile Coué.

*   *   *

Text: Maziar Raein

Where there is passion & desire, there will always be new horizons.

Graphic Magazine
Issue Six

Editors
Marc-A Valli
 Editor-in-Chief
 marc@magmabooks.com
Lachlan Blackley
 Features Editor
 lachlan@magmabooks.com
Samuel Baker
Sebastian Campos
Mairi Duthie
Inca Starzinsky

Design
Samuel Baker
Sebastian Campos (Aficionado)
Inca Starzinsky

Publisher
Rudolf van Wezel

Production
Rietje van Vreden

Advertising & Marketing
Mairi Duthie
T +44 7780 707 004

Printing
Drukkerij Tuijtel
Hardinxveld-Giessendam
The Netherlands

Paper
For this edition the paper choice has been selected
from the international assortment of Schneider
Papier Benelux. For more information please visit
www.schneider-papier.nl

Luxocard I, 250gsm
by Cartiere Burgo
[one-sided SBS-Board]
 Cover
Luxo Pak Silk, 150gsm
by Stora Enso
[practically woodfree silk coated art paper]
 pp1–96
Planospeed, 120gsm, volume 1.32
[woodfree offset paper,
made from Eucalyptus fibres]
 pp97–128
BVS Plus Gloss, 150gsm
by Scheufelen
[woodfree gloss coated art paper]
 pp129–160
Recystar, 150 gsm, volume 1.30
by Lenzing
[high bulk uncoated paper,
made from 100% recycled fibres]
 pp161–176

Addresses

Editorial
Graphic Magazine
c/o Magma
117–119 Clerkenwell Road
London, EC1R 5BY
United Kingdom
T +44 20 7242 9522
F +44 20 7242 9504
graphic@magmabooks.com
www.magmabooks.com

**Publishing, Subscriptions
and Advertising**
BIS Publishers
Herengracht 370–372
NL-1016 CH Amsterdam
The Netherlands
T +31 20 524 75 60
F +31 20 524 75 57
graphic@bispublishers.nl
www.bispublishers.nl

Subscription rates
(all prices include airmail)

1 year (4 issues)
 Europe: EUR80/£55
 USA/Canada: US$105
 Other countries: US$125

2 years (8 issues)
 Europe: EUR149/£103
 USA/Canada: US$195
 Other countries: US$225

Student subscription
(valid only with a copy of your
student registration form)

1 year (4 issues)
 Europe: EUR63/£43.50
 USA/Canada: US$90
 Other countries: US$100

How to subscribe?
Use the subscription card in the magazine or
mail, fax or e-mail us your name, company name,
(delivery) address, country & telephone/fax
number and the type of subscription you require.
Please include details of your credit card type,
number, expiry date and your signature. If paying by
Mastercard, please also add the CVC-2 code (last
3 digits of the number printed on the signature strip
of the credit card). If the delivery address is not the
same as the credit card's billing address please also
state the billing address. If you do not wish to pay by
credit card please mention that you wish to receive
an invoice. Your subscription will start after payment
is received.

A BIS Publishers Publication

ISSN 1569-4119
ISBN 90-6369-091-6

Copyright © 2004
BIS Publishers
Amsterdam, The Netherlands

BISPUBLISHERS

Editorial.

ALWAYS A GOOD TIME FOR GENOCIDE

By Marc-A Valli

'This ain't Rock 'n' Roll - this is Genocide'
David Bowie

If you watched television in the mid 80s you might still remember coming across these semi-naked figures lying listlessly in tents in the middle of the African desert. Exposed ribcages, swollen bellies, smooth black skin stretched over protuberant bones - these bodies could hardly be confused with the healthy bodies of the ads. Bulging eyes would stare at the camera while flies wondered about freely over sunken cheeks. Suddenly the eyes would blink. They were still alive. Though the flies looked livelier. You could hear them buzzing, loudly, to the point that you even wondered whether the buzzing had been added afterwards in the studio.

This was not the first time we had come across such bodies on our screens - before that, there were the camps, the Nazi camps, those camps… - but this was the first time we were seeing them in colour, live. And though I'm not sure the term 'live' was apt, this was clearly not the distant past, not World War II. This was our time, our world. Our war? Whose war was it? Who was responsible for this sunny version of Auschwitz? Who could we blame for this? Where were the Nazis now, now that we really needed them? Where were the Nazi guards, the grinning Polish onlookers, the ghostly culprits of the past?

They were dead - and there we were, sitting now-not-so-comfortably on our sofas armed with our remote controls. And despite the fact that the images often threatened to spoil dinner, we continued to watch them, distractedly, with the corner of our eyes.

Until someone had the guts to get up and do something about it. No, he didn't switch off the television, he didn't change channels or request that someone pass him the salt. Instead he decided to organize a concert. An immense concert. To our great surprise unprecedented numbers gathered in stadiums or stayed up all night in front of their televisions to watch the world's most prominent figures sing, wriggle their hips, wave, hug and kiss and congratulate themselves on their generosity.

This ain't Rock 'n' Roll, this is Generosity…

Live Aid was a sort of surreal climax, a celebration of the power of images on television. But generosity had its limits and afterwards everything went back to Rock 'n' Roll - in that part of the world in particular. Rwanda, Somalia, Congo, Liberia, Sierra Leone, Sudan… We kept discovering new African countries. Then came former Yugoslavia, former Soviet Union…Afghanistan… Our geography was severely tested as the cameras rolled on. Bruce Springsteen. Walls crumbling, towns in ruins, deserts being carpet bombed, missiles veering towards

WHERE WERE <u>YOU</u> IN 1984?

their targets, towers collapsing…Every day, every year, reality was presented to us as fields of debris, earthquakes, mass graves, burnt-up cars, crowds waving weapons and clouds of dust rising over the horizon while journalists held on to their microphones. If you tried to recreate a picture of the world based solely on what you were being shown on the news you would imagine a place filled with craters and sand and rocks and yellow dust - something akin to Mars. Was that reality? Was that for real?

But after years of this uninterrupted bombardment the viewers' habits began to change. When I was a kid my father used to rush home in order to catch the evening news and an austere silence would spread through the house as the programme started. Since then, however, more or less since the early 90s, audience figures for newscasts and other 'factual' programmes have been dropping steadily. Except for the occasional highlight (Iraq, 9/11, Iraq II, Saddam Hussein - The Sequel…) the audience was no longer paying any attention.

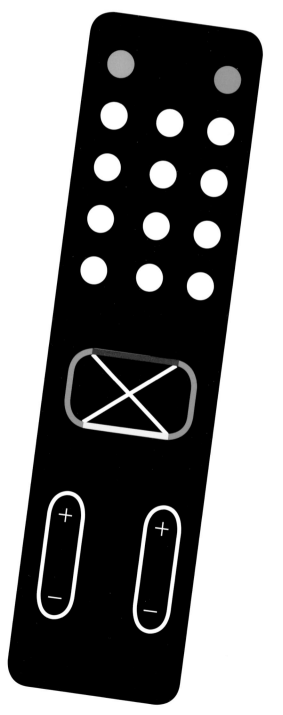

Then something unexpected happened. Tv, and in particular the notion of reality on tv, was rescued by a distant cousin, a poor relative: cctv. What took place was a very neat switch. From reality on tv - to reality-tv.

Viewers moved away from the pompous decorum of the news to watch how healthy young men and women brushed their teeth, talked in bed, prepared breakfast, fooled around a swimming-pool, sat endlessly, aimlessly in a room, chatting, gossiping…Viewers watched out for some suspect movement under a duvet or a sheet, a bare foot, naked shins, a bit of skin…Armies of makeover volunteers scoured the planet, bringing style and trends to backward populations, while back home, surveillance broadcasts allowed us to rediscover the lost charm of corridors, corners, angles & shadows as every moment of our lives was being filled with the excitement of being observed. The tv screen engaged us in a vaguely mythical journey. We were not searching for the Mystery of Life, but for some kind of mystery in some kind of life. Big Brother had become little brother, little brother walking down a dark corridor, trying to open one door, then another… How frustrating, all doors being locked, little brother went down on his knees and spied through the keyhole.

But guess what? Someone was holding a picture in front of the keyhole. What we were looking at was not reality - it was just the idea of reality, an idea, a vague idea. It just wasn't real. Reality is not the same as its reflection on a camera lens. And that's what I'm trying to get at. That reflection. The question of how we look at reality, how we react to reality, how we portray reality. It's by no means a trivial one. In fact, I believe all radical changes - in art, thought, society, politics, in our own lives… - come about via head-on collisions with reality.

One of my favourite examples is that of Italian Neorealist film. At the end of WW2, a generation of filmmakers found themselves faced with a strange and almost unthinkable reality. They felt it was their duty to explore it. But with the Cinecittà shut and Italy in ruins they no longer had the conditions to make films in they way had been taught to. So they invented a new way. This experiment gave us the films of Rossellini, Visconti, Da Sica, Fellini, Antonioni. Films capable of transcending the reality they were exploring. Films that would later inspire The French New Wave and continue to echo, all over the world, to this day, from the Battle of Algiers to City of God, via Mean Streets and Taxi Driver. Films which defined cinema as an art form, proper, as opposed to a form of mass-entertainment.

I looked away from the screen. It wasn't too dark yet. I could see the sunset reflected on the windows across the road. I heard the blasts produced by a television somewhere in the building. I heard hip-hop music bouncing off a car speeding on the road. I realised I was still alive and, despite being partly buried by the cushions of the sofa, I wondered what our next encounter with reality was going to be? When? Around which corner?

* * *

This issue's cover image is based on a project by
Less Rain [pp94—99]

Graphic Magazine

Issue Six
Revolutions

TOCtiontoc.

Graphic Magazine

Issue Six
Revolutions

Graphic Magazine

Issue Six
Revolutions

Show + Tell + Profile

Look / Read / Use

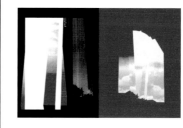

010

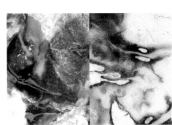

HAS FINDING THINGS BECOME MORE IMPORTANT
THAN THE THINGS THEMSELVES?

**Issue Six—Graphic Magazine
Contents**

Textfield IV

March 1st 2005, www.textfield.org

Photography by *Michael Wells*

2K BY GINGHAM

Artwork by Wythe Hansen

New York based group Faile was founded by Patrick McNeil, Aiko Nakagawa and Patrick Miller in 2000 within the idea of collaboration and exploration. Bringing together other artists and designers on various projects around the world, they continued these experiments with a series of highly original books.

Faile

Text by Lachlan Blackley

How did you form? Patrick McNeil and Patrick Miller have been long time friends going back to high school in Arizona. I don't think there was a time that we weren't swapping sketchbooks, collaborating on pieces or just talking about creating projects. We had always sort of talked about starting a studio together and kept in touch during art school courses in Minneapolis and New York. During that time McNeil and Aiko had met at a club in New York, where she was doing motion graphic work and McNeil was exhibiting paintings in the space. Feeling limited by just doing club work, Aiko was introduced by McNeil to the world of street art, and a new passion emerged. With the third member in place, our tentative ideas, based

01

around large-scale screen-printed illustrations, slowly began to come together in early 2000. I think we were always interested in the idea of an art group, similar to a band but as visual artists, where the work could really be made through the collaborative process.

What does the name 'Faile' signify? Faile began as Alife - a word that appeared in a sketchbook a long time ago. We began collaborating on a few screen-printing projects and after putting up a lot of work with the name Alife in NYC, we found that there was another Alife, a store/gallery on the lower east side. So we started thinking of what to call ourselves and what a name should possess. When we were putting up some work one night, we were arrested for posting artwork. As the long hours of waiting in the pale green cells

underneath Manhattan began to take their toll, we started to reflect on what it was that Alife (our Alife) was about, what quality that title possessed. This is when we were feeling low, feeling a bit defeated from the events that had transpired earlier in the evening. And it was there in the belly of the beast that Faile was realised. Faile is about this growth process - about taking your fears and your challenges, your grief and misfortune, and creating something from that. So we looked at Alife and by taking what we had, we created something new, something that was born out of Alife and became our own. ALIFE > FAILE. The name has really become not only a label (and in a business sort of way you could say a 'brand') but something that is born out of a place and time for us. And something that does have a philosophical

02

03

04

undercurrent, that flows through the work we do. Serendipity is another important aspect of this, because you never know where these growth opportunities are going to come from. It is exciting to us that there is this slightly intangible quality to the work. We hope that the viewer can interpret the work in a variety of ways, that there is some kind of spark there whether it is identified or not.

You collaborate with other artists, designers, photographers, writers and musicians. What do you most like about this way of working? It is hard to say what makes collaborating a great working process. There are so many good aspects to it. I believe we are really attracted to process. Looking at doing things in different ways. Looking at how different people interpret different ideas. It

makes us grow to see someone extend themselves and push something in a different direction than we would have initially chosen. That is really the best part about collaborating, the exchange of ideas and processes when working within certain parameters.

How does living and working in NYC activate Faile ideas? Well, first of all NYC is so intense in terms of its energy and the people that live here. Every one is on the hustle, always exchanging new ideas and projects. There is never a lack of projects to work on here, so it keeps us really busy. It's a dream city, nothing seems impossible in NY. It really is what you make of it and I think we apply that same idea to Faile.

You've published 3 books 'Orange', 'Death' and 'Boredom' and you're about to release a fourth -

'Lavender'. Can you explain a little about the ideas and people behind each book? The books in a way serve as two functions for us. One is that they give us a chance to work with people that inspire us and second is they kind of act as a yearbook for us. We do a lot of travelling and along the way we meet a lot of talented people. The books kind of give us the opportunity to tie every one together under one theme and to see what happens. The themes are not what make the book; it is the people in the books. The themes that we choose are often chosen quite randomly. In each book we try to mix it up a bit bringing together people from around the world and all different backgrounds from music, writing, fine art, street art, photography, to design.

Your work also focuses on direct public contact by plastering

05

06

07

the streets. Can you explain further your street projects and installations? Well, in the beginning this was true. Having taken a few notes from the OBEY campaign, the idea was to wheat paste the shit out of cities and get up as much as possible to get the name out and to make our mark so to speak. Another reason was the pure enjoyment of what was going on in the streets and wanting to be part of that. But, things have changed a bit since we first started. It has become less about the public seeing it everywhere and a bit more personal. I don't think we care about getting tons of stuff up like we used to. For one we have not really wheat pasted in a year now. We like to find a couple of nice spots and do a really nice job on them. All the work we have done on the streets lately is painted with a brush and then stencilled. I feel it

is much more personal and artistic in a way. There is a nice permanence to paint that you don't get with a poster. Sometimes I felt when we were putting up posters that it was kind of like putting up advertisements, it kind of lost the fun and energy that I use to get out of it. I don't know, I really look at the street as more of a canvas now. I like to work there but it is more personal and less about trying to get work up. I really hate all the bullshit beef that goes along with working in the street, but I enjoy working there and seeing the changes.

Can you tell me more about the images you work with? In the last 5 years we have built a small library of images, a set of rather whimsical and eccentric characters. They've come together in a variety of ways, bits and pieces that have been sampled and created from here

or there, to create a dialogue with their viewers. The more successful Faile images do this. They seem to have a little story that they're involved in. Hopefully making the viewer ponder where this character is and what is really happening. Now a lot of this is intentional, in the beginning it was more serendipitous. We try to incorporate the idea of duality with our images. Mixing a variety of images and messages to show something both positive and negative. Some have a very direct effect like the Dog, which sorta grabs you by the balls. Whereas the Bunny Boy and Girl offer something more curious and inquisitive.

How important is travelling and working globally for you? It is very important. It opens you up to new people, cultures and ideas; it keeps the creative juices flowing. It is also great in terms of work.

08

01
Bunny Boy

02
10 Ways

03
Untitled painting

04
Dog

05
Faile Mary

06-08
LA Paintings

We not only get the opportunity to work with people in America but it gives us the opportunity to have different projects going on all around the world. From a creative and business stand point it is the most important aspect of Faile. Working globally gives us a much broader base to work from.

Tell us about Faile fashion? Faile's roots are in design so because of that we are open to any projects that concern any aspect of design, fashion included. We often apply images we have used on the street but a lot of the time when we do a fashion project we are designing specifically for that project and it has nothing to do with what you see on the street. It is just another challenge for us, and a way to keep things interesting.

What projects are you working on at the moment or planned for this

year? Currently we are working on a few different things. We are working with Walrus magazine of Toronto, to create a crest system to be used throughout their magazine. We are working with Tomato and a few others on the Duran Duran album artwork for their upcoming album 'Astronaut' And we have been working with Asics Onitsuka Tiger line, creating two new shoes (mens/womens) along with a toy.

> It makes us grow to see someone extend themselves and push something in a different direction than we would have initially chosen. That is really the best part about collaborating, the exchange of ideas and processes

How about the political nature of your work? Generally our work tends not to be too political in nature. We're still finding our voice. The medium of street art is political, some voices are louder than others but the message is the same, it's about getting out and expressing one's ideas in public. Artists are getting arrested for this. One thing that we have used in past posters was the phrase 'War Against Terror'. The media used it when the war in Iraq was about to start. We used it because we wanted people to think about it. The idea if war against terror seemed like a double negative, both sounded bad to us - like the idea of going to war with Iraq. Another thing we did recently was to curate an anti-Bush postcard pack with www.downtownfor democracy.org. We got other artists

like Futura and KAWS involved and put together a nice collection that's available now through D4D. The proceeds go towards raising voter awareness.

What is revolutionary for Faile? Do you consider yourselves urban revolutionaries in some way? I don't think we consider ourselves revolutionary. I think we are a part of a really interesting time in art and design where people are using their work and voice to get out there in ways that bypass a more traditional route. By working directly on the street we have been able to go around the conventional gallery circuit and let people see our work first hand in their daily routine. It lets a wider audience see the work whether they're aware of it or not. And pair that with the internet and global travel being so easy, there is something that is happening now that I am not sure has existed before. Artists today are able to show their work anywhere at anytime through the internet. This becomes a huge extension to exhibiting work for the public and as a means of exposure. You can carry out work on the street and start building awareness about that work. And then the internet makes it possible for people to contact and connect to you, and see an even broader cross-section of your work. Seeing the way the business world is starting to understand the impact of having good design and art in their product is really bringing the artist/designer to a much more valued level. I think it is just a shift. A new time that ushers in new methods to getting your work into the world. Of course in the end the work still needs to have a certain quality and charm to succeed but at least the avenues for starting out are a little broader.

* * *

www.faile.net

IF A PICTURE IS WORTH A THOUSAND WORDS, WHAT'S A <u>SLOGAN</u> WORTH?

Issue Six—Graphic Magazine
Show+Tell+Profile

What particular chemistry makes a person able both to dream things up and to make them happen?

Living by the book

Text by Mairi Duthie

Michael Mack is the man behind many notable books and most recently the publisher of SteidlMack, a new imprint publishing 'high quality art books'. When we met in a quiet and low-key Soho members' club, and leafed through the impressive products of year-one of his new imprint, Mack was concerned that we concentrate on the books he produces and the reality of the way he works rather on himself as an individual. At the risk of embarrassing a naturally self-effacing man I would say that, on a personal level, Michael Mack possesses a winning combination in more ways than one; a mixture of character traits that is both engaging and successful. He is described as rigorous, pragmatic and a 'real details man' by those he has worked with, while at the same time being admired for his 'intelligence and sensitivity'.

Mack took a circuitous route to arrive at his present role as 'book maker'. Initially he qualified in Law, and spent two stifled years as a Commercial lawyer in a high-flying City firm before escaping into the arts. Looking back, he doesn't regret having studied Law 'it is really useful from an analytical perspective and helps with clarity in thinking, writing and in having an organised and structured approach. It really does come up a lot in what I do now, I handle all my own contracts and deal with issues relating to copyright and intellectual property.' Nevertheless, he did need to flee what

felt like a hostile environment, and the first phase of his new life was working at Zelda Cheatle's photography gallery. Whilst getting involved in a series of exhibition-related items, from catalogues to fully-fledged monographs Michael Mack felt a strong gravitational pull to further collaborative work in print and production (rather than acting as a dealer/curator in a gallery or museum setting.) 'For about 10 years I worked as a freelancer, curator and a writer producing books, and effectively I had got to the point where I wanted to control everything, so that I could work with the artist, design the book, make the book with them and then find a publisher.' Mack developed a role that elided that of editor, designer and publisher - different aspects coming to the fore on a given project. Books made in that capacity include, Surface: Contemporary Photographic Practice (Booth-Clibborn) and Reconstructing Space: Architecture in Recent German Photography (Architectural Association)

During this period an important relationship was to develop. 'Many of the books I worked on were printed and published by this extraordinary man, Gerhard Steidl who started in the seventies in Germany working with Joseph Beuys. As a photographer he documented the works of Beuys and his contemporaries, then began collaborating even further as a silk-screen printer, before buying a wet-offset press and opening his publishing house. He is more than a friend and mentor because he makes all these books possible, creating not just the freedom from some of the traditional publishing constraints to make the proper book suited to each project, but also the intellectual space combined with rigorous standards which allow you to push and explore the boundaries in making books.' As a publisher, Steidl is unusual in that he has a noble tradition of work with cultural and socially-concerned luminaries- mixing literary and socio-political roots with more fine-art concerns, including a notable relationship with Gunter Grass, which stretches back to the early days of the company's inception. Steidl, as a publishing company, are also unusual in keeping 100% control of print production, having

'one press from which all the books roll'. Mack recounts an anecdote in which he and Gerhard Steidl were experiencing a tricky time on press; with a technical hiccup threatening the desired result of the author. Standing by the inky presses, Steidl said 'If an artist leaves here and is unhappy then we have failed.' It is for this reason that many top photographers seek out Steidl to sit and work closely on their books, rather than handing precious work off to disappear into a vacuum.

So a strong affinity and shared emphasis on collaborative work with artists and writers led to Mack joining the Steidl 'family' in 2003, as managing director of the Steidl Illustrated books division and founder of SteidlMack. Mack started with a very specific notion in relation to his own imprint which is 'to make books which are the work itself…The perfect scenario for me is if people make work specifically for application to a book. For example, I am working with the painter, Andrew Grassie whose works are like photographic reproductions, and he is re-creating an art catalogue in a series of paintings, which will then be reproduced as our book. So the book format is used to confound and distort notions of originality and 'aura'. We try to apply the ideals of an artist's book to our projects, but without the inconvenience of poor distribution and inaccessible prices.'

As mentioned earlier, Michael Mack asked us to concentrate on his output rather than himself, saying 'it is all about books'. It does seem clear, however, that the books themselves owe their existence to Mack's own blend of 'applied' creative energy, which gives momentum to the process of making the books and has clear sight of the end result.

In year one of SteidlMack, books such as Paul Graham's 'American Night' and Clare Richardson's 'Harlemville' [01] dealt with gritty social observation of the dispossessed of middle of America. These works about people and society contrast with the third book on the 2003 list, Neil Drabble's 'Tree Tops High' [02], which visits the simple and pure human-free world of trees. The final work in that list, 'Insult to Injury' shows Jake and Dinos Chapman's manipulations of

Goya, which are simultaneously macabre and cartoonish, with a deliberate tension whereby the viewer is attracted and repulsed in a stirring way. The introduction to the book itself (by Jake Chapman) is almost comically impenetrable; thick with heavy concepts, allusions and arcane vocabulary. The impact of the whole, however, is compelling, and stays with you.

We try to apply the ideals of an artist's book to our projects, but without the inconvenience of poor distribution and inaccessible prices

In fact, all of Michael Mack's books are haunting, and not necessarily in a spooky way. The books create lingering echoes. They might make you notice something new or see a familiar sight from a different angle. You can see that one thing that Mack gets out of the whole exercise is the joy of taking part in an act of creation. He relishes the diversity of involvement with people of very different standpoints, and sums it all up quite simply; 'It is very exciting to work with extraordinary people and make books.'

Two of the projects in the pipeline illustrate Mack's work with very different writers/ artists. Anders Edström is a photographer with a delicate touch and a disinclination to express himself in other media, whereas John Warwicker is exploring words, images, different artistic forms of expression in an eddy of memories and theories.

Mack describes John Warwicker as 'having great powers of analysis, and great clarity and lucidity, but he also has one of those brains which contains a jumbled-up mix of things, which he can pluck out at any time. His referencing is extraordinary,

01

02

which is very much what his book is about. You can see all these layers being filtered through in a way that is all encompassing. It's hardly ever linear at all. Suddenly he drops things, then dives back to them which makes him not just exciting in conversation, but in working on the manuscript, where the draft of an entire chapter can change fundamentally because of one tiny thing.'

'Most editors would find this dementing,' John Warwicker cheerfully admits. 'The way I do books can seem ludicrously convoluted because the work continuously shapes itself, it's always in flux. It is not a question of just dropping something into a template.'

You can see all these layers being filtered through in a way that is all encompassing

One can see the attraction of working with Warwicker when, animatedly, he describes his approach as akin to work on a musical score, where change at any point could impact on the rest. Despite having to wrestle with something requiring almost infinite delicate calibration, Warwicker and Mack have eased the weighty structure along, working together towards a final resolution.

If you think of a film or a novel, it might describe events from a neutral standpoint, narrating things as they happen, or it might take a particular character's point-of-view seeing the action through their eyes. Going a step further, *The Floating World: Ukiyo-e* almost seems to project Warwicker himself without a narrative to relate. Rather than tying to 'explain' it, a few glimpses of the book itself are given here with the words of its maker to give a flavour of what the 400 page plus experience will entail.

01-02
'I look on this book as a container of thoughts and ideas. And with this thought comes the idea of inter-relationship and fluidity. Its a notebook to myself. Closer to sculpture than modernist "graphic design". Closer to hypertext or an 17th century book than a conventional book in that its not about linearity but flow and personal navigation with nodes or signposts rather than a journey from a to b.'

'Throughout "the Floating World" I've appropriated symbols from various branches of Mathematics. The symbolic function of some of these is closely related to the function origins others are used because they graphically represent my intended function rather than the mathematical function that they originally symbolised. This relates to my grandfather's notebooks and my fascination with the equations within. To me they seemed to be an arcane and poetic language. My grandfather tried to explain what these equations meant but unfortunately I wasn't sufficiently adept at calculus when I was 8 years old!'

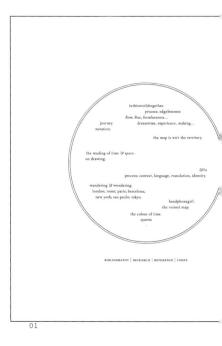

01

02

03
'One of my favourite films is Jean Cocteau's "l'Orphee". I first saw it when I was 16 at my school's film club. And I was and still remain entranced by it. And Thinking about Joseph Campbell - hero with a thousand faces…The idea that on every street there is an "Orpheus and Euridyce". This led me to think about my own journeys through cities and the cities I love…And how I "read" them.'

'each moment of seeing holds a shape
or line, the slope of a shoulder, the angle
of the foot, the momentum of an
elbow…criss-crossing, interweaving…
a turning away or passing through.
never draining more than the moment.
an accumulation of marks…forming a
crowd once more. all within the terms
of the drawing and not as an illustration'

'For years I've struggled with
drawing in the city/urban environment and then in Barcelona
I realised that the people were
like the waves in my sea/river
drawings…'

CONTENTS

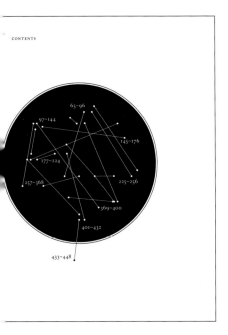
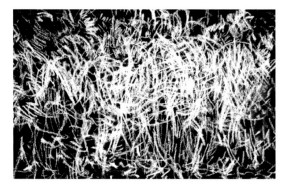

each moment of seeing holds a shape
or line. the slope of a shoulder, the angle
of the foot, the momentum of an
elbow… criss-crossing, inter~weaving…
a turning away or passing through.
never drawing more than the moment.
an accumulation of marks… forming a
crowd once more. all within the terms
of the drawing and not as *an illustration*.

Ramalleres, Barcelona.
Chalk on Paper, 21cm x 15cm. 2001.

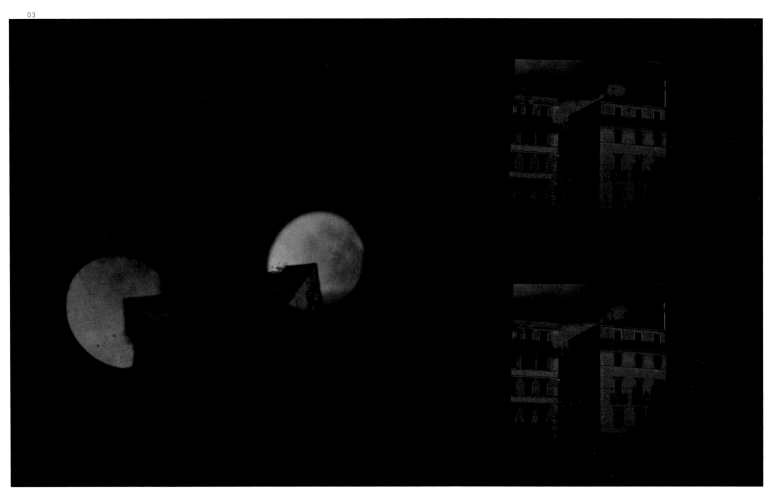

In contrast to the floating universe of The Floating World, Anders Edstrom's two books arrived at Steidl Mack almost fully formed. It required a different kind of input from the publisher. Michael Mack 'took to the work, as it is really quite unusual, particularly in the way in which the images are anti the idea of the decisive moment and against the notion of 'beauty' and challenge the 'fact' that the photographic frame can encompass something conclusive.'

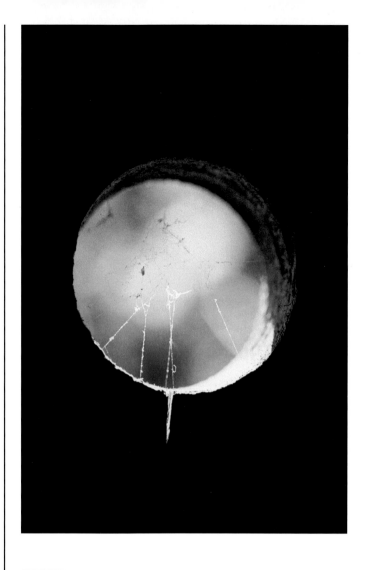

The selection for these books was based on what I felt comfortable with as a group, and what felt right at the time

The two men had known each other before, and had explored the possibility of working on an earlier project together which proved impossible. This type of relationship, where one thing (although failed, in this case) might lead to another is a common feature of Mack's work in publishing, and one that he compares to the typically long-term relationship of gallery and artist.

The books are called: _waiting some birds a bus a woman spidernets places a crew_

The elliptical titles are deliberate, or at least they were not intended as a tight definition of the contents and were added after the collections were put together. You will find images of birds in the first volume and images illustrating the concept of 'waiting' in the second. Edstrom says, 'I hate themes. For me it is not always the individual images that are interesting, but the way they work together… The selection for these books was based on what I felt comfortable with as a group, and what felt right at the time.'

In one slim volume you may chance upon a man in a mac and tie wandering down the street, looking

down, almost as if his eyes were tight shut, but it's his floppy white hair which catches your attention, and reminds you of something you think you recognise from a couple of pages back. Yes, it's him - there he is, clutching his coat tightly around him and stroking one ear, further back along the pavement. So despite the lack of themes there are some dreamy trails, with enigmatic links of time place or person.

'Some groups of pictures were originally taken in sequence, so they might be numbers 1,2,3 and 4 on a roll, but sometimes those sequences may be interrupted.'

Despite an un-precious approach to his work, Edstrom found the task of selecting pictures really difficult. 'It took me a long time I found it very hard to do. But in fact it took me a long time to have the courage to sit down and do it, then it took one or two hours.' During the build-up to getting the dreaded task done, Edström had made 'some rules' for himself and was 'quite methodical' in order to tackle a choice from 'several hundred photographs'. One rule was the use of a selection of small sequences. When you flick through the images, which seem so free and uncontained you may spot or imagine other hidden links or just go with the flow and take them as they are.

* * *

Books (in order of appearance):
American Night by Paul Graham
Harlemville by Clare Richardson
Tree Tops Tall by Neil Drabble
Insult to Injury by Jake & Dinos Chapman
The Floating World: Ukiyo-e by John Warwicker
waiting some birds a bus a woman spidernet places a crew by Anders Edström

www.steidlmack.com

023

ARE THERE ANY DECISIVE MOMENTS <u>LEFT</u> FOR PHOTOGRAPHERS TO CAPTURE?

Issue Six—Graphic Magazine Show + Tell + Profile

Suspended in a gallery or moving with a dancer on stage or film, Sandra Bamminger's costumes begin and evolve with the idea of motion. Her cheeky wearable pieces of art bounce like springs and flap like sheets of mulberry paper from the House of Boing.

HOUSE OF BOING

Text by Lachlan Blackley

What is the House of Boing? The name is closely related to where I take the inspiration for the clothes: kinetics - the art of the moving sculpture. I have always been interested in the interaction and relation between the wearer and their clothing. What would happen if the clothes had a life of their own? What would happen if their dresses would move by themselves, independent of the wearer? What would be the wearer's reaction? Would they stop to move, or change their movements accordingly? Would the wearer's characteristics perhaps be more openly visible through this improvised, instant reaction to motion? So 'boing' suggests this movement, a bouncing sound, like jumping, like wobbling, flapping, extracting, and contracting. We wanted the website to be a cosy place for people to meet for strange clothes and new collaborations, hence 'the house of'.

01

Can you tell us a little about your background? I initially came to the country from Austria for one year only, to do a BTEC diploma in Art & Design at the Eastbourne College of Arts & Technology near Brighton. I studied all 3-dimensional sculpture techniques but specialised in textiles and clothes construction. I like the interaction and enthusiasm in artistic circles in this country and decided to stay. I then applied to the Central Saint Martins college in London for a BA in womenswear and completed the course in 2000.

Have you always made clothing? One of my earliest memories is turning round-and-round-and-round staring up at the glaring sun till I fell over. That used to be my test for a 'good skirt'. If it was wide and light enough to stick out horizontally, I liked it and that's all I used to wear as a girl. This rounds up my interest in clothes till I discovered my enthusiasm for creating sculptures from soft materials and eventually ended up with the first idea of bouncy skirts and dresses.

How do you define your pieces? Costume, Art, Clothing? House of Boing clothes have the potential to be all of the above. Through their movement they are obviously very suitable for costumes in dance pieces but also to dramatize characters in plays and generally in performance of all kinds. They can be shown and treated as art when they are displayed hanging static in a gallery as body sculptures, or handed out and used in performances and interactive workshops. They can also be viewed as objects reconnecting us to that childlike enthusiasm and curiosity, an instant reaction to new and exciting objects and activities that a majority of 'adults' have lost somewhere along the way. Above all I really want the clothes to be accessible to people. It should be possible to look at them for a bit of unusual visual entertainment and stimulation in live performances and films (and on the internet). But more importantly I'd like as many of the clothes tried on and tested by the public, experimented with, dressed up in, tried on a with a different personality ...

Do you make them yourself? What's the process of design and construction? At this stage I make all the clothes myself. I am starting to use a computerized knitting machine to facilitate production. The process of design and construction usually follows a new idea of motion. After coming across an old forgotten textile technique or image of a new sculpture or a new material, I usually try to envisage a new style of moving dress. The design process tends to be foreseen and predicted only to a certain point. The dress has to be made and 'born', as only by looking at the finished product can I learn more about how to facilitate and change designs according to what's needed for the current collection or commissions.

I'd like as many of the clothes tried on and tested by the public, experimented with, dressed up in, tried on a with a different personality

What are the ideas behind your concertina style? My first idea of a moving dress was a bouncing one. I wanted to construct a jumping skirt through the use of elastic materials and a technique which enables the clothes to expand and then jump back up by themselves. Since then I have explored different techniques responsible for other movements - the flapping like a book of mulberry paper, the spinning of suspended crochet spirals, the wobble of crinoline rested on homemade spirals ... Motion brings the design into existence. The idea of the motion construction comes first. If there's a pleasing design but not enough motion, it's usually responded to with a complete redesign.

What are your influences and sources of inspiration? All 3-dimensional movement inspires - floating objects on the river, clouds, currents, waves, windmills, balloons, kites, toys, gadgets. But also sculpture, usually kinetic or set designs. Often 20s and Bauhaus. Finding old books on long-forgotten arts like rug-weaving in the Himalayas or crochet in Hungary or cross-stitch in Venezuela will often inspire and remind me to look at things with different possibilities in mind. Animation, especially early kinetic scratched films by Len Lye and his theories on doodling really held my interest for a long time. Sometimes I look at sculpture from the Bauhaus till now. I adore Schlemmer and his eccentric stage and costume designs and ideas. I love Calder's mobile sculptures, Duchamp's Rotary Wheels (which are bases for some of the new tutu collection). Naum Gabo's heads and rotating string sculptures …

The dance film was the result of the desire to exaggerate the comicalness and cheek in the dresses; I wanted to show them in a slapstick manner, easily accessible and understood

Where would you like to go with your work? Theatre and film? Dance? Fashion? Even though I am not necessarily interested in the fashion world and its fashion weeks and shows I would like my clothes to be available, which is why I will continue to have events in this field. I would always like to pair the dance and fashion, either present new collections in collaborative dance pieces or find dance groups interested in collaborating in my shows. I would very much like to explore further theatre and set design and eventually bigger and better funded film projects.

You've just made a dance for film piece. What led you to working with dance and film? Is it a better way to show the costumes in motion? Ever since I have made moving clothes I have experimented with ways of displaying their activities to make it instantly visible what they do. Photographs can give you the impression of motion, but why not have actual movement if you can? The dance film was the result of a desire to exaggerate the comicalness and cheek in the dresses; I wanted to show them in a slapstick comedy manner, easily accessible and understood. Through film we are able to show the impossible in combination with the possibilities moving clothes offer. I am always looking for new rhythms and music that gives you the urge to dance and sets up the atmosphere and mood of a space. During the process of the film I had a lot of opportunity to play with music in combination with projections and set design inhabited by dancers (in dresses that move by themselves and with the dancer). John Lindquist and I have been working on a way to capture the nature of the dance lighting with three different coloured lights and shadows on film. We half-lit jumping figures to accentuate the dramatic moment of the take-off and to give the clothes a little more sinister and darker quality even though they are mostly bright or light coloured.

Are you working on anything at the moment? I am currently working on a collection to be presented at the Viennese 'Museums Quarter', one of the biggest art exhibition spaces in Europe. An all white and yellow collection will be complemented with a cartoony kaleidoscopic dance film completed in collaboration with video artist Angeliki Xirokosta this summer. The score was also composed especially for the film and the fashion show by Paul Flanagan who will also set the mood for a chill-out party after the show.

Tell us about your collaboration with Tina Tahir. My collaborations with Tina Tahir explore various ways to display motion with photography. We have shot a series of photos to be displayed in flipbooks so that people can appreciate the actual bounce up-and-down of the dress. We have experimented with jumping sequences and double exposures to illustrate

the movement of the dress as well as freezing the moment of no return, the moment of defying gravity.

What else would you like to explore? I would very much like to work with people of all other disciplines of movement, more acrobats, wheel gymnasts, swimmers, snowboarders, skaters, bikers … In the nearer future I would like to increase my costume clientele and set up a hiring business. There are also plans to set up kids' dance classes in collaboration with Indian, African, Caribbean and belly dancing tutors involving moving dresses as part of the class.

* * *

www.houseofboing.com
www.tinatahir.com
johnlindquist@hotmail.com

02

01
<u>Comic Strip</u>, a dance film sponsored
by the Austrian Cultural Institute
photography by John Lindquist

02
White kinetic crinoline spring skirt
1646 gallery, The Hague,
The Netherlands

03, 04
White classic, Blue flower and
Burgundy apron hemp flap with
mulberry paper skirt.
All dresses are made with sustain-
ability in mind.

03

04

ARE <u>RAGS</u> THE NEW RICHES?

Aya Ben Ron places the disturbing medical imagery of bodies and organs within the decorative. Seducing the viewer to images of pain and discomfort, her work undermines the scientific and medical treatment of the human body, revealing it as a form of physical torture.

Aya Ben Ron
Text by Lachlan Blackley

Can you explain the ideas behind your work? I choose images that try to bring something to light, some scientific truth. This impulse to expose the 'truth' is completely intermingled with the pleasure of seeing. Visual pleasure is combined with the desire to seek the 'truth'. I would like the viewer to be in the same position. He has to look for something in the piece and to feel some pleasure while watching it, but then to fall into the abyss of his own desire, to what triggered it in the first place, that is the will to know, to understand, which has more to do with darkness than with light.

Have you always been interested in these themes? Although I've always been interested in these ideas, I'm still not capable to explain specifically how I was inspired to these themes. People usually tend to think that I'm suffering from some mental or

Issue Six—Graphic Magazine
Show + Tell + profile

IS THERE A CURE FOR MODERN MEDICINE?

physical illness. Well, I'm not, however not as far as I know. I guess that I get something from hanging in between what we consider (or are educated to see as) the normal and the pathological.

What led you to work as an artist? Are the beginnings of your ideas in the stuff you did as a kid? I was born in Israel, did gymnastics, music, dance and army service and I became an artist by decision. As for the beginning of my ideas, some of my best childhood memories are from the time I was spending at my grandmother's hospital (she was a gynaecologist), running around the corridors, sneaking into patients rooms, eating hospital meatballs with the cook and waiting for her to finish working and taking me home.

Where did you study? Goldsmiths College, London (MA Fine Art)

You depict western medical imagery in an eastern way. Why is this? Western medicine and what it represents and offers to us is the ultimate contradiction to the eastern way of thinking. I'm

01

02

fascinated by the paradoxical attempt of stitching them together.

Can you explain further the use of the mandala in your work? Mandalas are meant to serve as aids for meditation, to serve as an aid to concentration. The combination of the mandala's structure with the medical images, offers a coherent and well-organized structure and at the same time, exposes it as a fraud.

Can you explain your technique? The images are taken from scientific and medical textbooks and manuals, and then digitally redrawn on the computer as line-art images. The different styles of representation of the original images, which derive from different media (photography, drawing, lithography, engraving), are erased in favor of a clean and even line.

Western medicine and what it represents and offers to us is the ultimate contradiction to the eastern way of thinking. I'm fascinated by the paradoxical attempt of stitching them together

---

What inspires you creatively? Professional medical books and First Aid books, hospitals, suicide bombers, IDF, Japanese and Korean cinema - directors such as Miike Takashi, Kim Ki-Duk, Fukasaku Kinji, history of medicine and science museums, the holocaust, the political situation, my friends.

Tell us about your work 'Hanging'? 'Hanging' was made while I was artist in residence at the Wellcome Trust. It's a permanent site-specific work installed in the Wellcome Trust building. The work (25m long) is suspended inside the building's stairwell (5 floors)

01, 02
Hanging
Double sided print on fiberglass fabric.
120cm x 2500cm
2001

Wellcome Trust Building, London, UK Hanging (edition 1/3) is a permanent site-specific installation, suspended from floor to ceiling in the foyer of the Wellcome Building, headquarters of the Wellcome Trust.

03-06
4 Seasons 2002
Print on paper, foam tape. (Each piece contains approx. 7 layers, which are glued one on top of each other to create a 3D pop-up effect)
73cm x 86cm (each)
2002

This series of 4 pieces is inspired by four multi-layered copperplate engravings entitled 'The 4 Seasons of Humanity' (1680) which present a cross section of the history of medicine and science up to the 17th century.

04-06
Details of 4 Seasons 2002, seasons 2, 3 and 4

03

04

05

06

and in order to be viewed in its complete form, the viewer needs to either go up or down stairs. As an artist 'implanted' at the heart of an institution, which is dedicated to the research and preservation of pure scientific and medical knowledge, I was interested in making a piece that would operate as a malignant tumor within this structure. My idea was to produce a piece that would look astonishing enough to get the permission to hang it at the core of the 'temple of knowledge'. But while hanging, the piece would undermine or contaminate the purity of its hosting body - the Wellcome Building. In the piece, images of medical procedures look like physical tortures. What is actually a legitimate medical treatment seems like an intense violence directed on the body.

And '4 Seasons'? This series of 4 pieces is an 'updated' version of 'The 4 Seasons of Humanity' (1680) which are 4 multi-layered ('fugitive sheets') copperplate engravings that present a cross section of the history of medicine and science up to the 17th century. 'Fugitive sheets' is a pseudo multi-dimensional image constructed from carefully cut figures and body organs, superimposed on a basic illustration and often with an overlay illustration. The result is an illustration that can be 'peeled off' so the interior can be inspected by the viewer. Each of my 4 seasons is made out of 7 layers, which are glued one on top of the other with foam between the layers to create a pop-up effect. No need to peel anything off and no interior can be inspected.

What are you currently working on? A series of clay sculptures and 2 short videos (4 minutes long) about 2 procedures. The first procedure is anaesthesia and the second is the cleaning of an operating room.

Future ideas? I would like to put up a live runway show, in which the models demonstrate different first-aid transportation techniques. And to live in Japan.

* * *

033

Violence and nature. Guns, castles, office workers, mountains, volcanoes, warring couples. Using symbols to create an odd sense of unease, Kevin Christy's mixed media drawings often explore the strained relationship between the organic confined in a corporate environment.

KEVIN CHRISTY

Text by Lachlan Blackley

When did you start drawing the kind of things you do? Did it begin as a kid or is it a style that developed later? As far as the imagery I am working with now, it's mostly things I have developed lately. But some of it is definitely a nod to being fourteen and drawing nerdy boy stuff.

What is your background and training? I went to Art Center College of design in Los Angeles. I was born and raised in a suburb of L.A. called La Crescenta, and I currently live in Burbank.

What do you like most about being an artist in L.A? The community of people out here have a lot of enthusiasm. There is not as much art-wise (compared to say New York) so the people are very appreciative of it when they can see it.

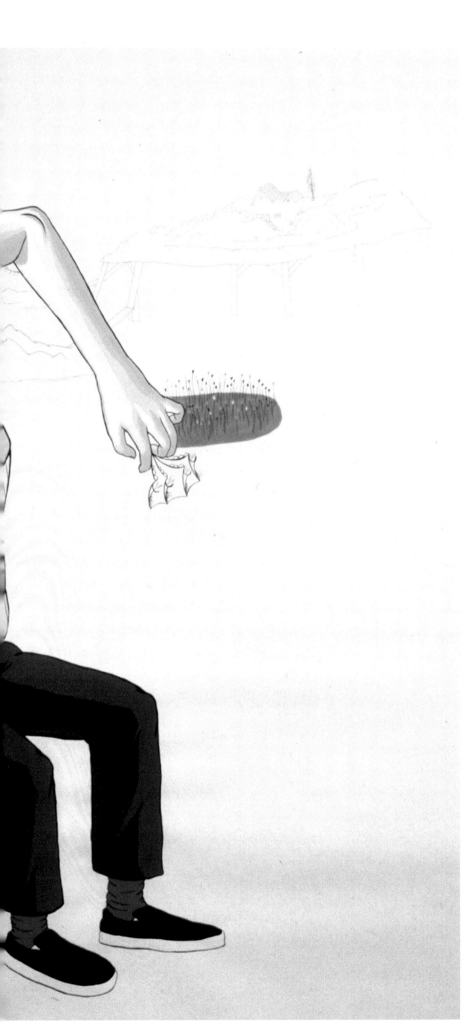

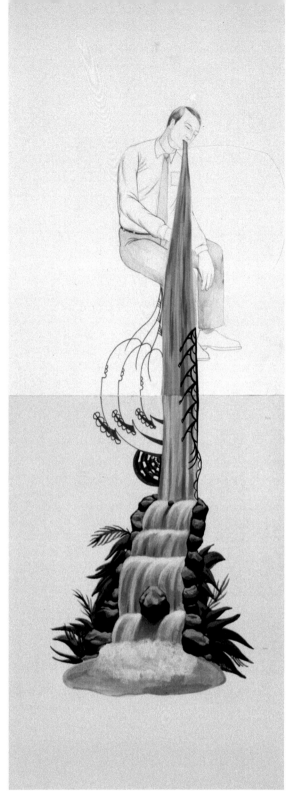

02

01
Woman Running

02
Waterfall

Where do your images come from? All the imagery I use comes from my surroundings mostly. I try to use the imagery of my surroundings as symbols to get across my concepts. The guns and the violence aren't things I literally come in contact with but they are undeniable, especially lately. I use certain things like mountains to symbolize achievement and brick walls to symbolize systematic organization. The goal is to juxtapose them against elements that are more chaotic and less defined to create a sense of uneasiness. I am fascinated by the idea of confining something organic like a human or a plant or an animal in a corporate environment. It's interesting to me how we react to certain types of organisation. What are the by-products of that situation? It's not necessarily a negative thing, it's just a thing, it's a reality of our current living.

I am fascinated by the idea of confining something organic in a corporate environment. It's interesting to me how we react to certain types of organisation

Is there a deliberate recurring theme or message within your work? I think the theme of my work is examining the hierarchy of different situations, both natural and un-natural. My work is an examination of the inherent competitiveness in life, and how living and non-living things relate to that competition.

What inspires you creatively? I have a need to make stuff, I can't tell you why. I'm really inspired by normal life. The average events that make up all our lives. The types of things we all have in common, love, disappointment, achievement, fear. The things that make us similar.

03

04

05

Issue Six—Graphic Magazine
Show+Tell+Profile

WILL THE EVERYDAY SURVIVE THE EVERYWHERE?

06

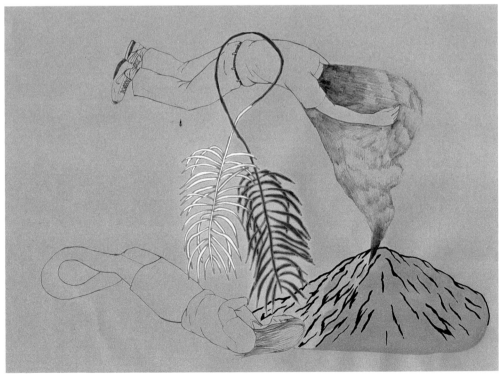

07

05
Prida & Joy

06
Unequal Relationship

07
Untitled

Has anyone made a huge impact on what you do as an artist? I admire a lot of artists to be honest, but the ones that have had the most impact on me are Jason Holley, the Clayton Brothers, Taylor McKimens, Misaki Kiwai, Ashley Macomber, and Rich Jacobs. They all have a truly great attitude about what it is to make art and to be an artist.

What's your preferred medium? I primarily use gouache and pencil. When I work larger I use house paint. I have been making large paintings in the last year or so (around 10 feet x 10 feet). It's really fun and the imagery takes on a new feeling when it gets that large.

I'm really inspired by normal life. The average events that make up all our lives

What projects are you working on or planning for this year? I am painting right now for two shows I have in December of 2004. One is a solo show at Richard Heller gallery in L.A. and the other is a group show in Philadelphia at space 1026. And I just started working with the 'Plea for Peace' foundation to raise money for a teen centre that will teach kids art and music. We're working with artists to create products to sell, with all the proceeds going to the teen centre. We're very excited. Also my company 'the broken wrist project' is coming out with a new book very soon on New York artist Misaki Kiwai.

Can you tell us more about 'the broken wrist project'? Any plans to publish a book on your own work? The broken wrist project is something I started in college. It's basically a publishing company and an artist collective. We put on shows and do book projects together. I'm the creative director and James Hughes is the editor. Our first two books are illustrated short stories and features on young artists. It's something I am very proud of. We're really lucky to have two great

08

09

10

Issue Six—Graphic Magazine
Show+Tell+Profile

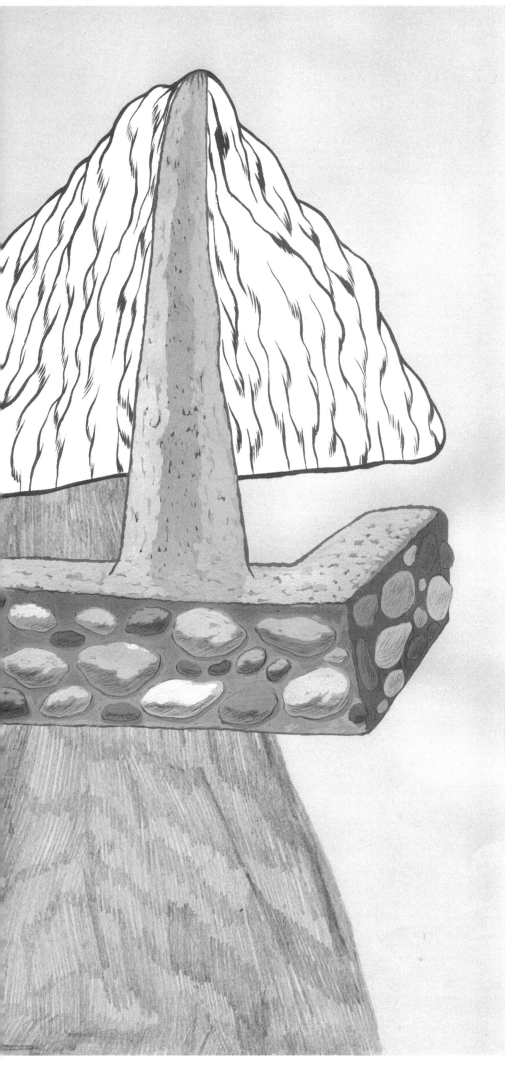

designers (Brett Kilroe and Tracy Boychuk) who make the books look super rad. My work appears in some of the books but I don't have any plans on doing a full fledged book on myself.

It's an interesting time to be alive and I think it's an artist's responsibility to interpret that

What would you most like to explore in the future? I would just like to keep examining the human condition in reference to the situation that is being a human being in the modern world. It's an interesting time to be alive and I think it's an artist's responsibility to interpret that. *Why do you think it's an interesting time and especially for an artist?* I think that the world is both getting smaller and larger simultaneously. Technology is so overwhelming that people are both being seduced by it and trying to fight against it at the same time. You can see it in art as well. New art is being made with new mediums while at the same time people are wanting to see work that clearly shows the hand of the artist in it. It's most exciting to me when they're side by side. It's the co-existence of the two that is so interesting. It feels to me like the world is in a transitional period.

Issue 06 is the 'Revolution' issue. What is revolutionary for you? Revolutionary is just being unafraid to live by your own accord. It's the practical application of the realization that you can do things however you choose to. It's being stoked, and not feeling embarrassed about it. Fuck 'em, do what you want.

* * *

www.kevinsayshi.com

Her mum calls her a 'general specialist' … the multi-skilled Lizzie Finn combines a passion for 70s handcraft manu-als with dig-ital technol-ogy to produce unique fabric illustration and graphic de-sign. Armed with a sewing ma-chine and a Mac, Lizzie hints to the nostalgia of macrame days.

Lizzie Finn

Text by Lachlan Blackley

Were you always drawing or making things as a kid? Both my parents are quite creative. My dad was a graphic designer and I used to go with him to work and draw around French curves and use old bits of Letraset and things like that. My mum used to make stuff and she'd get me modelling bits of play dough. And I did a lot of drawing - my mum said that my drawing was really good until I went to school, and then I started to draw like everyone else! At school I didn't really enjoy art classes at all, so I never thought I'd do anything to do with art and design. I chose to do maths and computer science at A-level and I thought I'd do art as a kind of antidote to that, but I ended up becoming completely into it.

What led you to graphic design? On my foundation course I didn't

01

MOLOKO

PURE PLEASURE SEEKER

02

IF YOU HAV

A cross to be

03

really know what to do. I was really thinking about doing everything - fashion, fine art. And I chose graphic design because I could see that you could carry on using whatever materials you wanted. I saw a lot of this 3D work around, and the idea that you weren't expected to just work in one way was quite appealing.

So when did you begin working with fabric? I think the first time I used it was just before I started my degree in graphic design at Central St. Martins College. We were asked to make a self portrait on the first day we came in and I made a small patchwork thing because I'd seen an exhibition of contemporary art quilts at the Craft Council, which was really inspiring. I think the reason I liked it was the fact that it was using something different in the context of graphic design. I was drawn to it because of the way it was constructed together, but also because it seemed like something really different and had a similar quality to the Pop Art stuff in a way … sort of 2D with the 3rd dimension added to it.

I wanted to use craft and I wanted to use them in a very graphic way

What really kick-started the move in this direction for you? After I graduated I made three posters that were fabric stretched onto large frames for 'Holmes', the company that became Silas. And about the time I was doing that, I went to see Paul Neale from GTF who was one of my tutors at college. He'd seen that I'd been working in fabric and that I was into craft and things, so they commissioned me to do a double page spread image for them, for a section page in the book '20th Century Type'. They'd been given the 70s and they asked me to come up with something using 70s typefaces that were handicrafts, because they'd been thinking that was a good association. I came up with the idea of doing bookmarks, which they liked. So I made these bookmarks

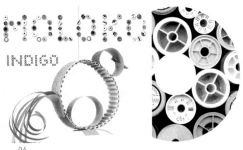

04

05

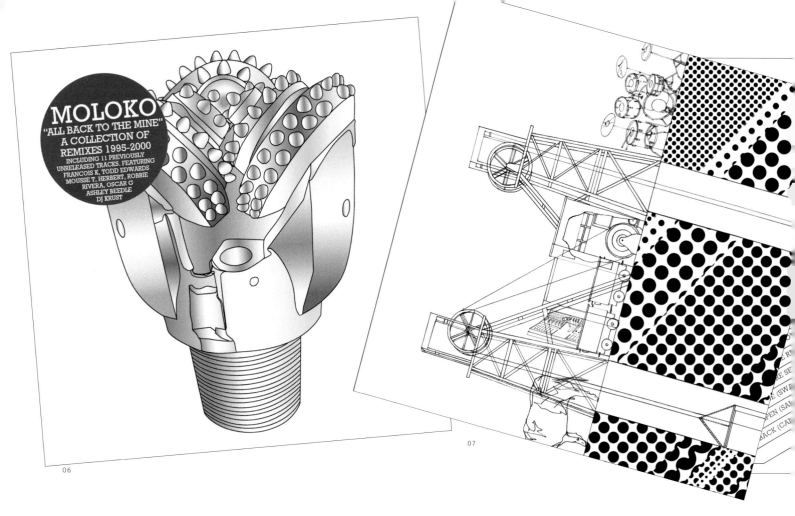

MOLOKO
"ALL BACK TO THE MINE"
A COLLECTION OF
REMIXES 1995-2000
INCLUDING 11 PREVIOUSLY
UNRELEASED TRACKS. FEATURING
FRANCOIS K, TODD EDWARDS
MOUSSE T, HERBERT, ROBBIE
RIVERA, OSCAR G
ASHLEY BEEDLE
DJ KRUST

06

07

and then it was really with their process of working, which was to photograph them on a copy stand, with the idea of creating type and image from a photograph in an old-fashioned layout kind of way. That was really influential because I've worked in this way quite a few times since then.

What do you like about working with the handcraft and the digital? I think a lot of this was simply trying to be different to what was around at the time. When I was at college there was quite a lot of stuff being done with computers and everything seemed to be much more digital. I think I just really wanted to distance myself a bit from that. There was also this sort of naïve child illustration and I didn't want to be a part of that either. I wanted to use craft and I wanted to use them in a very graphic way. *Do you like that personal hands-on feel to it?* Yeah I think I do, there's just something interesting about seeing the structure of something. I'm not actually sure what it is that I like about it … it just seems to work for me. And I don't always use it for graphic design. I've done a lot of work in this way as illustration but I like to think that I can also work in different ways. For instance for

the Silas book I kind of put the two things together, the graphic design thing and some of the illustration stuff that I've been doing. So it's kind of using graphic language and making it into something else.

How did the Moloko cover for 'Thing to Make and Do' come about? A few years after I graduated I set up a studio with Ben Sansbury, Robert Green and Marcus James. We all put our work together and started showing people. One of the people I went to see was Elaine Constantine, a photographer who photographed Roisin Murphy from Moloko. She recommended that I send them my work because they were looking for a designer at the time for that album. A lot of the time you have to pitch for these things and this was just a case of 'we like your work and we want you to design our record cover', which was really nice. They did have input into the design but they gave me a lot of creative freedom. Luckily they had good taste and good ideas and the record company trusted their judgement, so it worked really well. And I've since realised how unique a situation that is! *Did it grab attention for you?* Well, yes and no. I didn't just suddenly get loads of work from it, really. I think that's when I

started doing more of the sewing illustrations. Instead of going on to design more record sleeves I started creating imagery as opposed to graphic design, and I started to design the T-prints for Silas as well. But on the back of that I did do the Beta Band album and single. They basically came to me with what they wanted and I generated it for them.

Generally how do clients approach you? Do they have an idea of what they want from you? I think lately if it's illustration, it's usually because they've seen something, and they want it to be like something that I've done. I don't see that as a bad thing really because it's a point of reference to base things. Sometimes I think it's good to ask people which pieces of work they actually like because in my portfolio there are quite a few different approaches, and I think unless I find out which ones they actually like I could end up going down the wrong route for them. *Do you like having the freedom to come up with the whole concept or working in collaboration?* I generally like to have control over things and I like to collaborate on things only when it's quite clear cut who's doing what. I really

08

liked working with Clare Price who directed the Nokia 'Fashion House'. She commissioned me to work with her to create an animated version of my illustrations. It was really nice to see it all happen; working in postproduction and with all those things I don't have time to actually learn to do myself. *So how was this done?* Basically it was first shot as live action and then recreated digitally. We worked fairly closely together although a lot of it was a process where everyone sort of goes away, does their bit and gets together when they need to, which was quite nice and a good sort of teamwork. Which I don't often do, often I'm just here working away on my own and doing everything myself. *What did you like about seeing your work in animated form?* It was just pretty amazing, partly for the simple thrill of seeing your work on TV. And to see it transferred from being what it is, a piece of fabric done on a sewing machine, to seeing it moving on a TV screen.

What's the general process from idea to finished piece? I got into the habit of using drawings to develop an idea and I still do that. I tend to come up with the idea in sketchbook and then at some point I get onto the computer. If I am doing

something with sewing I tend to work everything out on the computer and then transfer it onto fabric and then I'll have that photographed and then sometimes I'll do something in Photoshop or on the computer again. I do like that simplicity when something's been photographed, that's the artwork, that's the finished thing.

A lot of the time you have to pitch for these things and this was just a case of 'We like your work and we want you to design our record cover'

Can you talk a little about the influence of 70s and 80s craft manuals? What attracted you to them?

I think from an aesthetic point of view they differ greatly. Some of them are quite slickly done, but most of them tend to have quite grainy photographs showing the objects that have been made. I love the warmth of the design, the photography and the diagrams. And the language that's used - words like 'haberdashery' and 'macramé', you know, these kinds of things - they just have this ancient sound to them. But I realised that the thing I love most about them is this kind of hopefulness of things that you might want to get around to doing. And that kind of idyllic world where you don't have to work, you just sort of sit around making things and then hanging them up in the house. And I think it is the fact that they're quite welcoming, the whole idea of them is to include people I suppose. I think that's why I like any kind of manual, it's designed to be accessible and that's definitely something that appeals to me.

What sparks your ideas and imagination? What do you look at to get ideas? Books definitely play a part, for various reasons. Sometimes you can flick through a book and it will be the design that gives you an idea and other times it can be the way it's printed or something

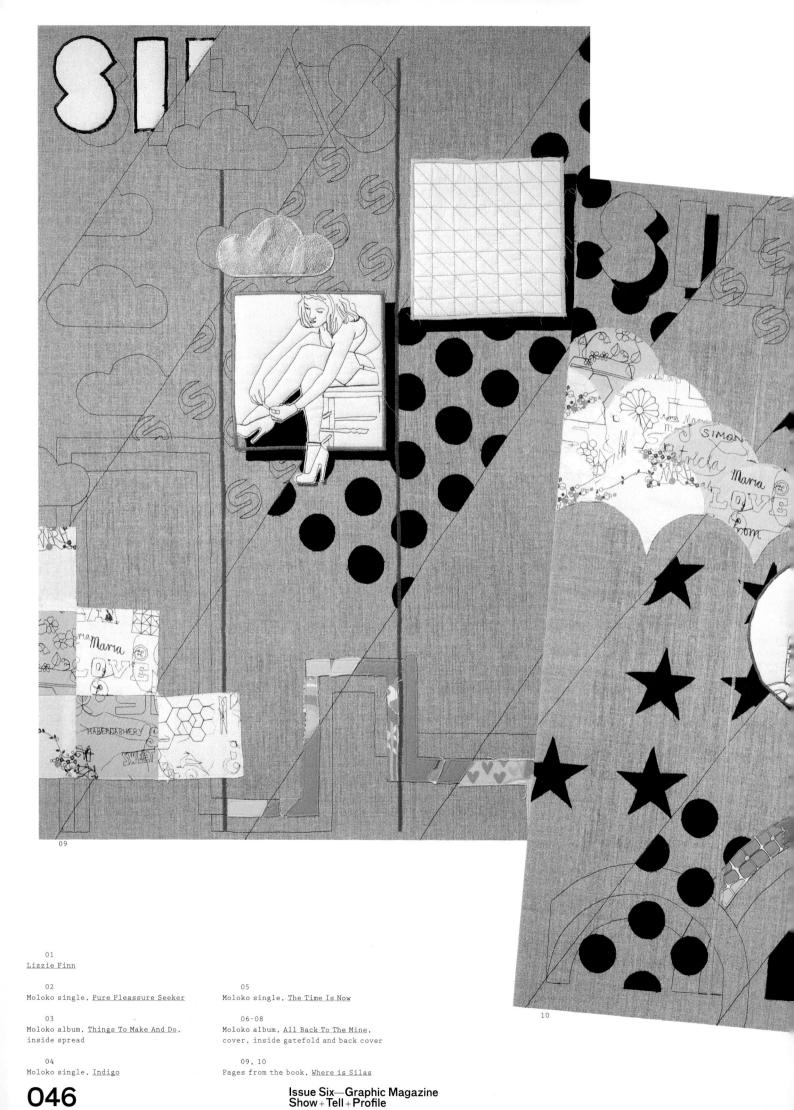

09

10

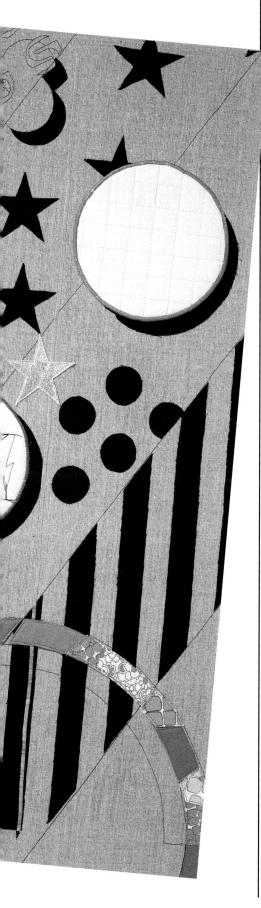

about the photography. I find looking through books really helps me. When I was at college I used to spend hours and hours in the library looking at old books about all different kinds of things. I often find it inspiring to look at the stuff that isn't graphic design and then bring that into the design. Or then maybe look at other graphic design and change it some way. I have a lot of books and I tend to buy them all the time.

Have there been or are there other artists that made an impact on you? Yeah I think GTF's work had quite a big effect on me, partly because Paul Neale was one of my tutors early on and his attitude towards design was quite influential. After I graduated I'd often see things that they'd done and be really jealous and wished that I'd done them! But generally it was the mood of it. Our way of thinking at the time was a bit similar to what they'd already been working on - we'd been thinking along the same lines. Also I was quite influenced by my peers at college. There was a feeling of wanting to do something new and prove something to one another. And I really loved Joseph Müller-Brockmann's work. Then later I got into Herb Lubalin and Milton Glaser … Milton Glaser I really love.

Because it has a kind of hands-on look to it, and you can see what it's made of and how it's done, maybe that's comforting in some way?

Why do you think people are attracted to the style that you work in? Because it has a kind of hands-on look to it, and you can see what it's made of and how it's done, maybe that's comforting in some way? A lot of imagery can be quite manipulated in an invisible way with a lot of retouching so maybe it's a bit of

an antidote to that. But then I'm not sure, because I'm not against digital retouching either. I don't know, it's hard for me to see … *Do you think it's the familiarity or sense of nostalgia?* Yeah, I think nostalgia plays a big part. I'm a very sentimental, nostalgic person and I've always liked working with things that I feel somehow attached to, or feel like that they kind of belong to me somehow. I mean, I do like working with new things and new ways and using new technology but it does take me a while to feel like I have ownership of it or some kind of personal attachment to it. I think I'm happy when I'm bringing together ways of working that I'm really familiar with.

You've worked a lot with Silas. How did this relationship begin? It sort of began with Ben Sansbury who knew Russell and Sofi who formed Silas. When they started Silas I was beginning my design career. The first thing I did for them were these T-shirt prints, which I really liked doing. And I did these repeat prints. I think the first ones I did were in 1998. Then I did their catalogue for '99-'00 Autumn/Winter - I still really like that project. And they started using repeat fabrics for clothes and bags and stuff. So when Silas decided to produce a book, they had been working with a group of people who created work for them regularly. They'd become a kind of patron of the arts and design in a way, so they put a book together called 'Where is Silas?' with work from all these people. I had done anything I wanted basically, it was completely open, but I think in that situation I had to restrict myself by somehow making it graphic design. It's very, very loosely about graphic design, but I had to have some kind of format. So I chose a poster and it's one of my favourite pieces of recent work.

You've also done work with Frost French. Yeah, that came out really well. I was commissioned by them to do Art Nouveau pole dancers on a vest and knickers set. That was really good fun. It was an all-over print. I drew from a book of glamour models and I introduced these obvious Art Nouveau references to create a strange mix; you couldn't really see straight away what it was. And I did some other work for them, more repeat printed stuff. I'm not doing any more repeat prints at the moment, for Silas or anyone, really, but it's not something I've ruled out.

You're a bit of multi-tasker. Do you enjoy this way of working? Yeah, I like it and I don't. Sometimes I think it would be really nice to be very methodical and have a particular way of working. Because quite often I'm working with a different type of client and in a different medium, sometimes I do feel like I'm starting from scratch and back to square one. Which in some ways is really good, I think, because it means I'm not working in a formulaic way. But then sometimes I think it's good to have a formula! I think I tend to kind of do one thing and then move on to another and another. Sometimes I consider doing a needlework apprenticeship or something, because it's that thing of being 'Jack of all trades and master of none'! One thing my mum said once ... she asked her mum what doctor she'd gone to see at the hospital and she said she went to see a general specialist, which my mum thought was really funny. And she said that she could use that word to describe me - 'a general specialist'. Are you happy with that? Yeah, but I do think I have kind of limited it slightly. I mean I haven't tried to be a singer/songwriter ... yet. I've tried to keep it fairly limited. I have managed to do all these things since I graduated in 1996, so I have gained experience in at least these three or four things.

You also give college lectures and talks. What do you like about doing this? The first time I did it, it made me realise how much I'd learnt or how much I'd done. When you're working freelance or working on your own and you're just taking on project after project it's rare that you sit and take stock of what you've done and look through your work. And to see it up on the screen and to have to talk about it to a large group of people, it kind of distances you from it a little bit and helps you see it in another way. And it can be reassuring sometimes to say 'well actually I have done quite a lot of work'. Because sometimes you forget, it all gets packed away after you do each thing. And as a student myself I really enjoyed and got a lot out of hearing people speak. You know, whether I liked their work or not I

found it really fascinating to hear what they had to say. So I do think it's important to do that.

Sometimes I consider doing a needlework apprenticeship or something, because it's that thing of being 'Jack of all trades and master of none'!

What would you most like to do in the future? One thing that's been a constant since I started doing freelance work, is not ever really knowing what's next! So I never have much of a plan really. I can never really pinpoint what it is I'm doing, it just kind of comes along through choosing projects that have been offered. That seems to be the way of choosing what to do next. Are you inundated with projects? Yeah sometimes, and sometimes not. But I do get quite a lot of things that come along together and I have had people as work experience assistants before, but I'm not very good at delegating. I like to do everything myself, so I do get quite overwhelmed. Yeah, sometimes it's a bit too much.

*   *   *

www.lizziefinn.com

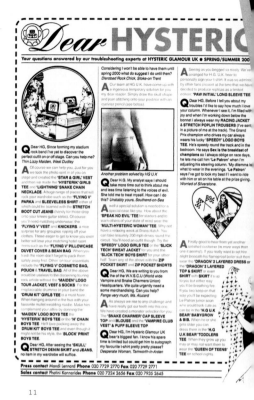

11

13

11, 12
Hysteric Glamour, promotional
leaflets

13
Selection of t-shirts and
prints for Silas

14
Silas exhibition poster, Tokyo

12

14

10 silas expo

LIZZIE FINN LIZZIE FINN
LIZZIE FINN LIZZIE FINN
LIZZIE FINN LIZZIE FINN
LIZZIE FINN LIZZIE FINN
LIZZIE FINN LIZZIE FINN

Dutch designer Tord Boontje's beautiful lighting, glassware, ceramics and furniture juxtapose naturalism and technology. Combining a passion for advanced materials and industrial technologies with a romantic aesthetic, Boontje produces contemporary products that bring a new sensuality into the home.

Tord Boontje

Text by Lachlan Blackley

What triggers your imagination? Well it's all over the place really … How I think of my work at the moment is this role of decoration and ornamentation with design. It's this ongoing discourse that started four years ago, where I started to really rethink the things I live with myself. And it starts with the question 'How do I see my home?'. For me home is not a white box to live in, it's something else much warmer. We have a child now, which very much changed my whole outlook on my home and I'm very interested

01

in the whole idea of decoration, this whole kind of sensuality, which I think we've lost in design. This is an ongoing question behind the work; it could be a new technology I haven't worked with before or a different material. A beautiful day in the park or a rainy day in the park!

I'm very interested in the whole idea of decoration, this whole kind of sensuality, which I think we've lost in design

Your work seems to be very nature inspired; it's very organic and romantic. Where does this come from? The inspiration comes from technology and culture as well as nature, but I chose to use a lot of natural motifs in the designs as a way of being very outspoken about the idea of decoration. If I was trying to do decoration with geometrical patterns there's much more to hide behind. I began with a collection of furniture called 'Rough and Ready', made of sticks and blankets and tapes all put together very, very rough and ready. And for this new body of work called 'Wednesday', which is about the everyday, I took one of the 'Rough and Ready' chairs, made a felt cover and embroidered a crow on it. We live in Peckham-Rye on the park in London and there are hundreds of crows, so it's something I could see from the window. It's something everyday for me, and something everybody immediately recognises as an image. Seeing how the embroidery worked on that chair, suddenly everything was possible - it was a kind of freedom. And the natural motifs really started to work as triggers for memory. As soon as we see a picture of a horse we all have our own stories and memories and fantasies that immediately get

02

03

triggered. Immediately you start to connect with fantasy. They're quite archetypal images. Yeah the first set of motives were crows, horses, bunnies, butterflies, dragonflies … things that we have in the park where we live. And now slowly, stranger creatures have started to creep into the park.

There's something folkloric and fairy tale here. Has this always been part of your imagination? No. My mother was a textile designer and a teacher of art history, so I grew up with a lot of art history around me and there was definitely an awareness of folk craft. But then in my own work it's only now that I've started to become interested in it. The more interested I become in technology and making things with machines, the more I become interested in making things by hand. And it's this whole duality between them. But I don't see what I'm doing as falling within a kind of folk tradition. For a start it was a very conscious decision to not use historical patterns for example, so we go to extreme lengths to make new patterns. Because I don't want it to be historical, I want to be forward looking, to be from now really. For me it's much better if I create my own imagery from scratch.

How do you go about designing your work or coming up with ideas? Is there a formula or is it quite spontaneous? No, it's very spontaneous. We do so many different projects and the nature of each one is very different. At the moment we probably have eight big projects running in the studio. One is work with ceramics, one is furniture, one is textile collection, and one is a lighting project. You try and do something new and you're kind of reinventing things or rediscovering things. So there isn't really a formula. Not for the first phase. I mean there's always an element of research that's usually part cultural and part technical in its nature. Because very often when you start making furniture - like now I'm working on a plastic chair and I've never worked on a plastic chair before - you have to learn about all the technical things. How do you do that? How do you go about that?

When you come up with an idea, do you just let the idea flow and think about how you will produce it later? It's usually in tandem. It varies a little bit whether they're projects I'm doing for myself or projects for a manufacturer or client who has asked for a specific product to be designed in a specific technology. So it's a different planning point. I get a lot of inspiration out of the techniques, out of the actual making. I'm very passionate about making - it's very interesting for me. So the technical and the cultural element of the work should be really fluid.

The more interested I become in technology and making things with machines, the more I become interested in making things by hand. And it's this whole duality between them

As a kid were you always making things? Yeah, I was always building huts and decorating my bike and stuff like that. In the shed at home we had our own workbench and we had our own tools as children and we could make things. My mother would enjoy sewing and working with textiles so she would make clothes. And when I was 15 or 16 I became interested in making my own clothes, so it's always been there, the kind of experimenting with things. *How did you decide which way to go in terms of studying? Why didn't you do fashion design instead of industrial design?* I might still take that up … No, I don't really know to be honest. I think when I was quite young I knew I wanted to work with products. I mean, I didn't know it in the definition I know it now, but I knew there was something there I wanted to do that was really interesting for me at 15.

What is your aim? What do you want to create within the home or for whoever is buying your products? Well I think I'm kind of selfish

01
Moroso exhibition

02
Midsummer Light is a lampshade made of two layers of cut Tyvek, a very strong synthetic paper, with a Mylar cone inside that keeps it away from the light bulb.

03
Chair featured in the Moroso exhibition

For me it's important that a product is very affordable - that if you see it and you like it, you can actually afford to buy it

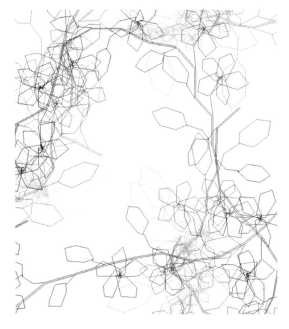

04

Midsummer Light
In the design process many models
were made and cut by hand to discover
the right pattern and shape. The chosen model was then scanned into the
computer and traced to make a digital
file for production, ensuring the
machine cut light has all the traces
from the handmade original.
Designed for Artecnica

05

Garland light. Laser-cut from a
single sheet of metal, the pattern
allows the user to wrap the Garland
around the bare light fitting as
desired. Produced by Habitat.

in that sense. I'm more concerned with following my own interests. So at the moment there's this whole question about decoration. Where does it fit in to our world? And if other people want to join that or are interested in that, then they're very welcome to share this thinking. But besides that I think if you're going to make a light it should give light and if you make a chair it should be comfortable to sit in … you know, just basic product qualities really. These are quite tricky questions because as soon as you start to ask questions about the user within industrial design there's a very fine line that you can cross and you're suddenly on the marketing side and on the side of marketing-led design, which I've never been a partaker in. It's always come from the other side. We all hope that what we make is a successful product. And very often for me it's important that a product is very affordable - that if you see it and you like it, you can actually afford to buy it. I mean, so much design exists in many things that never actually become part of real life.

It must make you happy that the Wednesday light can be produced by Habitat as the Garland light and made more accessible to the public? Yeah, absolutely. But for me it was never an aim to be the initial producer of the Wednesday light. It was more a necessity because nobody else was going to make it if I didn't make it myself. I'm sure now if I had made a beautiful drawing of it and gone to Habitat with that drawing and said 'Look, you can produce this. It's a light but it doesn't have a light box, so it's not really a light and it's not really a lampshade. It's a thing you add to a light that you already have at home. But you can sell it and lots of people will like it!', I'm sure they wouldn't have gone for it. But by actually doing it and not waiting …

Did you start out approaching companies with your product ideas? After I left college, I was designing exhibitions and designing shops and there was a moment when I decided I didn't want to do that any more, I wanted to work on product design. And sometimes I had a job with somebody and sometimes I didn't. I tried to send mailings out to companies I liked and companies I thought should work with me, but I'm very bad at those things and I

never got anywhere and I never got any replies. Then I thought well I'm going to change my attitude and I'm really not going to wait for somebody to give me a project or for clients to come by. And you don't need it. Probably if you're an architect you need clients to commission buildings but in the meantime you can also do your own work without being a practicing architect. And in industrial design it's much easier because you can actually think of really nice products that you believe in and start producing them. And then by producing them you can sell them and at least you're enjoying what you're doing. If you have good ideas, they will have a continuation and I strongly believe in that. There are a lot of projects that we start in the studio here without a client without a question, because I believe in them.

You do so much. Do you have a team of people in the studio that help you? Yeah, well today we have six or seven people in the studio. But that's a lot; it's more than normal. Usually it's like three or four people. There's Jodi the studio manager who really makes sure all the projects fit together in the timetable and everything is invoiced on time and she does all the communications. And then there are different designers with different skills. Some are very good at working on the computer and some are very good at hand drawing. Some are very good at specifically making things. So there's a combination of skills.

Do you find inspiration outside industrial design? Hugely. I mean you work inside contemporary culture so you need to be aware of contemporary culture. And for me I'd probably find art and fashion are the main source of inspiration. I look at that more than other design.

How did you enjoy teaching industrial design at the Royal College of Art? Well, I just did my last term because there's too much going on here in the studio at the moment. But I believe teaching is something you can go in and out of. For me it's also very much a social thing as well you know, to go out and talk with a whole other group of people about design and not about my work but about their work. It's a very enjoyable way to kind of think. In my last year with my students we had this topic of decoration

and technology, which is for me
an extended kind of research. You
had other people looking at it in a
completely different way than I do.
And fortunately none of the students
made many flower patterns this year;
they do completely different things.
But the work was very much looking
at the sensuality of objects and
using different senses like sounds
and smells and objects of smell.
So there's this fantastic kind of
dialogue that we have there.

*Do you enjoy the collaborative
process of working with other
designers or companies?* Yeah,
very much. When I work with other
designers it's really fantastic
to see somebody who you respect
and you've got this close insight
into the way that they work, their
approach, their opinion about
something. And with companies, if
they're good companies there's a huge
amount that you learn there.

*How did the 'Blossom'
chandelier develop through
Swarovski?* Swarovski had this
project called 'the Crystal Palace'
where they asked designers to
redesign or re-invent the chandelier
using Swarovksi crystal. Before that
I hadn't thought about crystal at
all. For me it was a very good match
because there is something about
the whole kind of brilliance and
light quality of crystal material
that really appeals to me. It's very
suitable for what I'm interested in
today.

*Can you explain the
Inflorescence project? What are
the ideas and technology behind
the process?* Inflorescence is a
collaborative project in progress
with digital artist Andrew Shoben
and computer programmer Andrew
Allenson. It's an experiment to see
how the computer can be programmed
to produce randomly generated floral
patterns. These drawings can then
be made physical by using other
digital processes, for example with
a computer-controlled embroidery
machine or digital printing, or 3-
dimensional by stereo lithography.

*With research into new
technologies and techniques, is
this something that you carry out
yourself or is it usually something
that you have access to through
working with bigger companies?* Both
really. At the moment I'm working
on a collection of textiles with
Kvadrat, a Danish company. I want
to do this photographic printing

06

07

08

06
Swarovski chandelier and swing chair

07, 08
Come Rain Come Shine
chandelier project

technique, which I know they're not doing at the moment and I think it might be possible but I'm not sure. So at the next stage I'll ask them to do research into that and as soon as they find out, we can become much more specific about it and then its kind of a joint research.

What I'm trying to do now is say ok, we can have this work which goes away from this cold, very neutral kind of modernism to something that's more humanist to live with

What for you is Revolutionary?
Well it's a big word 'revolution'. The way that I see it now, we're going through this third kind of industrial revolution at the moment. The first one was with the steam engine and the first factories. The second one was with the petrol car engine (well it wasn't until the 50's, 60's that we saw how the car changed the world enormously). And now we've just started with this whole digital revolution, which will hugely change the world that we live in as much as the previous ones. With the first one, when William Morris was working, he was very much working to find an alternative to industrialisation. Instead of using machines and very inhuman conditions, he thought we should make products in a very socially acceptable way and use the handcraft. Which probably made a lot of sense at the time. But what I'm trying to do now is say ok, we can have this work which kind of goes away from this cold very neutral, kind of modernism to something that's more humanist to live with. That can be produced in a very technically advanced way. Instead of going against technology I would much more go with technology. I think

there's a real kind of solution in there. *The way that you work seems to use technology without losing the personal touch.* Yeah, probably. But then we also live in a world that's so completely impersonal that maybe it's relatively easy to do something very personal? I don't know.

But there's another side to my work, which is the social side. For example I'm working with this group of women called Coopa Roca from Rocinha in the slums of Rio. Fifteen years ago they formed an embroidery co-operative of 150 women. They were selling work and embroidering at home but then they thought let's work together and let's earn some money. They've always worked for the local market and then earlier this year the British Council put Paul Smith, Agent Provocateur and myself in touch with them. So we've collaborated on a piece, 'Come Rain Come Shine' which was shown in Selfridges and this collaboration is like a starting point to work with these women. We made a big silk chandelier with them, which we're now developing into a more commercial product. The idea is that they will be the manufacturer. It's very luxurious, quite an expensive thing but its not mass produced it's very handmade. That's kind of an example where the technology isn't there, but it's trying to work in a different way with people. And it's probably something that started when my partner Emma Woffenden and I did the Transglass. We started to think about the whole recycling thing, working with a company that recycles and got local communities to bring empty bottles to the factory. For me the whole idea of manufacturing can be very empowering on a local level and there's something very positive about that.

Can you explain further the ideas behind the 'Happy Ever After' installation with Moroso? 'Happy Ever After' was an exhibition presented in the Moroso showroom during the Milan Furniture Fair in April. It was filled with ideas about nature and technology coming together. The materials, like the wool and silk fabrics are cut in such way that they create an organic atmosphere in the space - a space where things are hidden, waiting to be discovered. Another important inspiration for me is fashion and the way in which we use fabrics on our body. I try to bring some of

09

10

this sensuality to the designs.
I designed the series of seven
chairs as different characters
that you might meet in a story - the
princess, the pirate, the witch, the
prince, etc.

For me, the whole idea of manufacturing can be very empowering on a local level and there's something very positive about that

*How will the 'Forever'
collection differ from the 'Happy
Ever After' work?* The 'Forever'
collection is inspired by this
fascination with fashion. Each
piece consists of a core piece of
furniture with a changeable cover
made from couture fabrics. The main
difference between the two is that
Milan was showing the prototypes and
London is showing the pieces that
have been developed for commercial
production.
    Following the exhibition
of 'Forever' in London at the Aram
Store, Covent Garden (23rd Sept—
2nd Oct) there will be a selling
exhibition in NY in November at
Murray Moss's new gallery space
(next door to Moss on Greene St,
Soho NY).
    *What would you like to do most
in the future?* I don't know. I never
look that far ahead.

* * *

www.tordboontje.com

059

09
Rocking Chair

10
Embroidered chair featured in
Moroso exhibition

11
Tord with Babylon chair

GRAPHIC NEEDS YOU: WWW.GRAPHIC CULTURE.COM

Issue Six—Graphic Magazine
Look/Read/Use

Santiago Vanegas

Falling in love with Tracey, getting married and having a little boy together … *changed my life.*

I am from Colombia and I've been living in San Francisco since 2001. I don't talk much, so I make images. They are my voice. Images are born in my mind. Most of these images are impossible in the physical world. Because they are impossible, I must believe that they *are* possible. Only then can I create them.

Since 2001 I have contributed to Surface magazine (including being a winner of their 2002 Avant Guardian contest), Wiredmagazine, Flaunt magazine, Planet magazine, Tanqueray No. Ten, City magazine, Graphic magazine, Picture magazine, San Francisco magazine, and various Latin American publications.

068

Oh, say can you see … ?
27.06.2004

The images are about awareness, or a lack of it. The images are not about the awareness of airliners in the sky, especially post 9/11. They're about the unawareness of our ability to really do something, great or small, about our times. They are what I would hope to be a 'trigger' to a revolution. A catalyst.

[see also: Graphic 04, pp155-159]

Jon Burgerman

Being introduced to Photoshop when I was 17 … *changed my life.*

Jon Burgerman draws, paints, clicks and sleeps. Known for his scratchy and intermittently odd artwork, Jon works across a variety of media that includes painting, printmaking and computer animations. Jon has created a vast collection of strange creatures and amusing characters to inhabit his peculiar world of art which exists across websites, printed pages and exhibitions. Cynicism and confusion often tie his work together, building up a wider project linking together both his commercial endeavours and artistic ambitions.

Jon Burgerman's work has been published in various forms. These range from LP covers for Charles Webster and Winding Road Records to tee shirts, mobile phone animations and leatherette posters for Levis.

076

Religion
02.2004

A trawling scrawl of the tedium of parental-enforced religious belief. Boredom-lines intertwine religious iconography and sullen youths. The piece is a composite of a couple of drawings in felt pen and biro. It is quite rough around the edges as it was hastily put together through a fear of being struck down from above whilst working on it.

fries@jonburgerman.com
www.jonburgerman.com
www.biro-web.com

01

02

03

04

01
Character design
from www.jonburgerman.com

02
A3 digital litho print
sold as an edition of 60

03
Section from a hand drawn piece for the Wear It With Pride exhibition, September 2004, London.

04
Selection of stickers featuring characters from www.jonburgerman.com

Clarissa Tossin

Unexpected things always … *change my life.*

A' has been developed by the Brazilian designer Clarissa Tossin since the end of 2002.
A' was conceived as a one_woman_design_studio because the whole work process was developed by myself.
It is an analogy with the rock concept of 'one_man_band' when only one musician composes the songs and plays all the instruments.
Today A' works like a family where specific jobs are develop in partnership with different professionals.
A' is also a platform for graphic language's investigation into what makes sense once design pieces are a representative part of the whole cultural production of today.
Past and present clients include Vogue Brasil, MTV Brasil, MTV Latina, Rocket Racer Records (USA), Bizarre Music, Trama Records, São Paulo Fashion Week, O2 Films, Gullane Films, Vermelho Gallery, Die Gestalten Verlag (Berlin) and Liquid Frontiers (Austria).

078

Sky Boxes
2004

A photo collage series inspired by the sky reflection on the surfaces of glass-mirrored buildings.
The buildings seem to be made of clouds and at the same time they also seem to keep the sky as a prisoner of their own limits.

[see also: Graphic 04, pp148-154]

Look / Read / Use

Linda Zacks

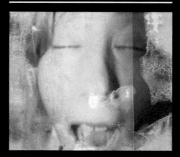

Eating that chocolate cupcake
… *changed my life.*

extra-oomph is a vibrant stew of
ooze. be loud, jazz it up, scribble,
gawk, listen to the paper as it tears,
colour outside the lines, find bliss-
ful jewels in the trash, reinvent,
suck every bit of juice out of the orange, see deep / think wide, feel the
movement in the streets, fling colours
towards the sky, collect cluttered
layers of yummy eye sludge, watch the
city decompose, vomit up the nonsense
and smile sweetly at the alphabet,
feel the breeze in the trees, float un-
derwater til you can't breathe, close
your eyes and scream at The Ridicu-
lousness of it all, smash crayons and
giggle, stare directly into the Sun,
snap, shoot, record Life as it whiz-
zes past your nose. Take all of it in,
inject the vibrancy, the surprises
the love, the conflict, the conversa-
tions / cry it out into a cup and then
drink it again … one shot from a shot
glass. extra-oomph is lindA zacks,
art chick and poet human, living in
brooklyn.

084
Recipe For Revolution.

This recipe is my take on what personal revolution means to me: the
radical changes and cerebral thunder-
storms when our innards are tossled,
unearthed, redefined, rebuilt, again
and again over the course of our
lives. While sprinkled with real
ingredients, like sweat, boundless
belief, soul sparks, internal and
external tensions, clenched fists,
wild eyes, time (it can take anywhere
from 2 seconds to a lifetime) and just
simply being a tumultuous personality with a beating heart, there
are also fictitious and whimsical
ingredients that make the whole thing
work - the little bits of magic that
make the recipe slightly different
for each human - so add sugar, some
rusty thumbtacks, spitballs, and the
right amount of swear words, one can
actually make these profound changes
happen. The crazy concoction doesn't
really exist, but if it did, it would
be something only made in Willy Won-
ka's Chocolate Factory.

linda@extra-oomph.com
www.extra-oomph.com

Frederique Daubal

Being a foreigner … *changed my life.*

French girl born south of France,
lived in different countries, travels
a lot and hates flying. Studied art and
literature, then design. Now based
in Paris. 3487 beauty spots. I like
green colour no matter what - wear
more dress than yesterday- send a lot
of SMS but I might stop tomorrow -
Love my colourful friends - I am still
a freelance graphic/textile designer
- drink red wine and sparkly water
- long weekend away are needed. Music
in my heart - I am working a lot to
develop my own pieces! And more. See
you - Wish you a happy November 2004.
Frédérique Daubal

frederique@daubal.com
www.daubal.com

088
Revolution Tranquille
Summer 2004

What make me getting up in the morning? My Little Revolution! Ah! Often
inspired by my behaviour, my friends
one, my soulmate, my son, my lovers,
people I meet once and never again,
or the one I talk to all the time in
my daily life … people … I am walking
the streets smiling thinking about
new projects. I am attracted by the
interaction between the needs and
the appearance of anyone, I confront
them to lead me to news point of view
or ideas. An outline dress for warm
evening?! A skirt made out of pockets
and belt to avoid bags and fit different sizes?! Could it be so uncool &
perfect to have a woollen body suit
for winter time?! … Temptation is
huge … I love tomorrow--- freder-
iqueDaubal

01

02

03

04

03

01
Faceless Tasteless America
part of a visual poem about the stars
and stripes

02
Jazzzzzzy!
illustration for Jazziz magazine

03
Woman BOX
holding 10 cards against breast
cancer

04
CAUTION
painting about that funky beast
called Woman

Less Rain

Less Rain … *changed my life.*

The Colony of Less Rain was founded in London in 1998 by Chairmen Alexiou and Eberle. Less Rain is guided by the twin principles of Progress and Humbleness, and our motto is: 'From Humbleness comes great things'. Less Rain has grown from a deserted and insignificant New Media Outpost into a blossoming International Organism, with factories in London, Berlin and Vienna and many prizes from our Leaders.

Comrades Schneider and Marusic played a significant role in defining the spiritual goals and visual leadership for our anti-precipitation campaign. Comrade Merrill composed our Great Hymn, which we hope will be sung by many future generations.

At Less Rain, the people of different nationalities, now in control of their own affairs, manifest enthusiasm for developing new media production and construction in many ways.

reception@lessrain.com
www.lessrain.co.uk

094
Say No To Bad Weather!
08.2004

Tina Marusic (Illustration)
Rose Merrill (Copy)
Lars Eberle and Carsten Schneider
(Illustration, Art Direction)

Revolutions are as inevitable and inexorable as rain. The campaign that we have devised is inspired by Chinese propaganda posters, however, it does not intend to make light of political revolutions in China or elsewhere - rather, we were inspired by the posters' surreal aesthetics and 'double speak' slogans, to create a parallel campaign based on an abstract, utopian ideal, drawing attention to the futility and silliness of imposing dogma upon others.

[see also: Graphic 04, pp56-61]

Ernst Fischer

Overalls … *changed my life.*

Ernst Fischer was born in Switzerland to creatively ambitious parents, both writers. After a spell at Zürich art school, he escaped to London to study film. He eventually abandoned moving for still images, attracted to their ambiguous nature. His work explores the interplay of fiction and documentary, of a sense of place and a point of view. 'Right now, I am interested in Hunter S. Thompson's hallucinatory style of reportage', Fischer says 'that hits the mark by missing the target, describing stuff that has no name. I'm working towards a visual version of that, something that might adequately combine speechless wonderment with unflinching realism.' He lives and works in London.

ernst@atlas.co.uk
www.webberrepresents.com

100
Not The Yellow Brick Road
06.2004

[see also: Graphic 01, pp82-87
& Graphic 02, pp162-169]

Mark Butcher

Ironing … *changed my life.*

Mark Butcher was born in 1979 on the Isle of Sheppy. In 1998 he started a BA in Visual Arts at Camberwell College of Arts. During his time there he worked on celebratory events for Emergency Exit Arts as an event artist, and built and designed lantern installations with children for events such as the Thames Festival and the opening of the Millennium Bridge.

Mark then went on to complete a course in Creative Arts Management at London College of Printing, where he gained experience setting up a number of Visual Arts Collectives, which allowed him to exhibit his own illustrations, paintings and installations around London. These exhibitions lead to him winning an award from a leading bank for 'Business Most Likely To Succeed'.

Mark works now as an illustrator/ visual artist and is employed by a leading children's charity as an event manager.

markbrixtonartcircle@yahoo.co.uk
markfuatch.moonfruit.com

01

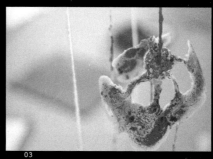

03

01
Eye
1999 Illustration

02
Body language
1999 Action not language

110
Egos
2004

Pages 110, 111
from left to right:
Decretum II, Decretum I, Vox II

Pages 112, 113
from left to right:
Geogoth movere, Inauguration III, Inauguration II
All illustrations are colour pencil on paper.

The characters in my painting are dealing with self-initiated anxiety. They are my alter egos. The images focus on the effects and the reactions of anxiety rather than the anxiety itself. It is difficult to place my alter egos in terms of age, gender and race, since they are singular characters fusing together the diversity encapsulated in all three. The alter egos demonstrate fear of sexuality, physical appearance, illness and status, which are all topics of reflection during childhood, adolescence and self-styled maturity.

Anxious occurrences lead me to occupy my time with domestic chores. Domestic meditative processes act as a placebo. Acknowledging that this process is not curative, but more of a distraction allows for the curing that comes in the form of the sinister humour. This is articulated in the depiction of my alter ego and my fascination with domestic organisation.

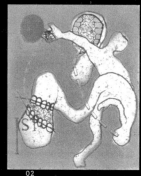

02

03
Self internal landscape II
2000 This installation deals with the desire to manipulate the internal human body in the same way we manipulate our landscapes.

Look/Read/Use

Matthias Gebhart

114

Pages 114, 115
Worshipping inner resistance,
Tag-age/Heart-ache

Pages 116, 117
Disturban weapons of mass confusion,
Me and my bucket of paint, watched by
a Bodé lizard

Pages 118, 119
The disturban sun is shining for all
of my children,
PSY and further inside bombings
06/07.2004

Writing graffiti … *changed my life.*

Born in 1972, started writing graffiti
in late 1988, bought his first Apple
Macintosh in 1996, started singing in
a punk/hardcore band in 1998, studied
visual communication at the University of Applied Sciences Dortmund.
Graduated in 2003. Lives in Western
Germany's former industrial heart,
the ruhr area, where you can't run
out of inspiration. Loves illustrating for records and magazines, books,
skateboards and everything else …

info@disturbanity.com
www.disturbanity.com

My design works are often strongly
influenced by the visual conception
of life I developed as a graffiti-
writer: very subjectively focused,
that means. I called it DISTUR-
BANIY, and it's about not respect-
ing boring surfaces, mentally,
visually, physically. The graphics
I contributed do actually contain
elements of my blackbooks, sketches
and photographs, including a REVOLT
silverpiece done under a bridge of
my hometown. Mainly they contain my
deep love for all kind of stuff that's
torn down and gets reused, redefined,
or just tagged over. It just comes.
Revolution is about radical change,
it's not about control …

01

02

03

04

01
Novum - World of Graphic Design
Title artwork, 2004

02
Evilove
Acrylic and spraypaint on canvas, 120
x 90 cm, 2003

03
Disturbanity
Detail of self-promotional CD cover,
2003

04
Nightcrawl
part of photo series, taken from The
book of Disturbanity, 2003

Florence Manlik

Conscience of the reversible character of most of the concepts … *changed
my life.*

This is it. The important question to
me, once that some work is achieved,
is: is this necessary? I mean, if it
wouldn't exist, would it miss? If
the answer is no, it goes straight to
the trash. If yes, then it will have
a chance to be shown to others, and
then, if they like it, it can exist
on surprising diverse support. The
last use who was proposed to me was
on snowboards. It is amusing. *A part
ça*, I'm French, living in Paris,
and looking forward for new
collaborations.

manlikflorence@yahoo.fr

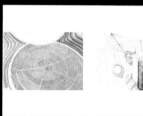

120

BISLAND

Page 120
flight over platform A
65 x 46 cm, 2001

Page 121
building
36 x 25, 2004

Page 122
more platforms
43 x 36 cm, 2003

Page 123
view from earth
70 x 43 cm, 2002

Page 124
explosion
23 x 26 cm, 2003

Page 125
catharsis building
86 x 70 cm, 2003

These drawings were part of my last
January exhibition called 'Bisland'. They are some kind of mental
landscapes. It 'happened' between
2000 and 2004. Bisland is not oni-
rique, it's like a horror B-movie,
quite sinister and funny at the same
time. It doesn't matter, nobody cares
about the subject anyway. Maybe it
is not fashionable. It does look like
nothingness, which isn't trendy for
sure. There is no temporality, it is
nowhere and everywhere, it is very
abstract. It is free, very personal.
It is an abstract activity, for an
abstract purpose. The thing is, it
had to be done.

[see also: Graphic 03, pp98-107]

Gustavo Lacerda

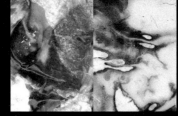

To accept the life ... *changed my life.*

What is here now, is already past.
The present is the place. Graduated
in Design at Pontifcia Universidade
Católica do Rio de Janeiro (1999).
Now doing a postgraduate degree in
Arts and Philosophy at the same
University.

gustavo@substantivo.net
www.substantivo.net

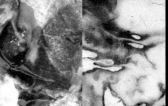

126
I like When I Recognise Myself
For Not Knowing Who I Am
12.08.2004

My ID card was washed away, by accident, changing my photograph
to a blur. My head, in the image,
exploded. This photo is my image to
the society, it represents me in my
documents, that says that I'm a citi-
zen. In a accident, this document,
goes, inside my pants to the washing
machine, and this image is destroyed.
Who am I now? The time, the accidents
and my life, are always asking to me
to reinvent myself, to become another
one, everyday. My life says to me:
'the way you were, you can't keep
going anymore.' And, if I struggle
to continue to be the same, if I fight
against the changes and the transformation, the result will be pain. But
if I accept it, and embrace the movement, I let myself be whatever my life
requires me to be. If I'm not so sure
of who I am, If I can live the situation instead of live myself, I make
the revolution inside of me, opening
space to any kind of life.

Niko Stumpo

Skateboarding ... *changed my life.*

Niko Stumpo was born in Drammen,
Norway. He grew up in the ice lands of
Norway, and at the age of 6 he moved
to Italy. and began vigorously skateboarding. Schooled in the field of
art, and later enrolled in a Fine Art
Academy, however never completed the
actual course. He has worked in different agencies all over the world.
Now he is in Amsterdam freelancing
for different clients on different
media. His artwork has been exhibited
at the Biennial in Tirana and Valen-
cia, the World Wide Web Exhibition in
Sao Paolo, Brazil, the George Pompi-
dou in Paris, the Riviera gallery in
Brooklin, NY, and the Witney Museum
in NY.

me@abnormalbehaviorchild.com
www.abnormalbehaviorchild.com

130
Untitled

I am always drawing and drawing ...
I draw little characters that remind
me of people I know, or I have met.
Everyone has his own character that I
try to show with little details.
It is about the people around me,
immersed into a strong summer sun
light. They come up into my mind while
drawing, never know where I
end up to. Just keep coming.

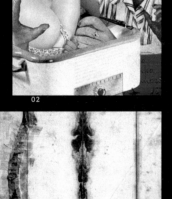

01
The little magic fairy from love

02
Young ladies who wants to be good
wives, must study the Scientia
Erotica Sexual Guide

03
My teacher of Tragedy and ancient
greek theatre, arrived at the class-
room, late with her hair in a mess,
but with her pride intact.

04
My spine: my father, my mother and me.

01
One of the illustartions for AIKO
clothing for their new 2005 collection.

02
Illustration for a Dutch T-shirt company called RAZKO, will be printed on
girls' t-shirts.

03
Illustration for a double spread on
Flavor Mag, a French magazine. It was
an article related to rock stars and
groupies.

04
Illustration for an Italian graffiti
magazine called Defrag.

Look/Read/Use

Mikko Rantanen

[She] … *changed my life.*

Mikko Rantanen is a graphic designer and illustrator. Originally from Finland, he is currently based in London after graduating from Central Saint Martins College of Art and Design in the summer of 2003.

After working at The Face and Adrenalin, Mikko has been working freelance for various clients including Arkitip, Lailatay and Tokion.

mikko-rantanen@jippii.fi
www.mikkorantanen.com

136
Boys and Girls
07.2004

Images about boys, girls and love

Albino

Growing up … *changed our lives.*

Ex-Central St Martins and Ravensbourne who originally met at Hereford Art College. Since graduating we've run a bedroom outfit outside of work hours doing projects that we invent, or jobs that find their way to us.

hello@albinoprojects.com
www.albinoprojects.com

140
Bed Revolution
08.2004

When thinking about revolution there's only two options: Black and red Ché imagery or beds.

[see also: Graphic 01, pp122-127]

01

03

02

04

05

01
Arkitip
Illustration for Arkitip

02
Rojo
Illustration for rojo

03
Tokion Illustration for tokion

04
Help
Personal project

05
Arkitip
Illustration for arkitip

Nikola Tosic

THE FUTURE IS DARK AND GRIM

146
The Future Is Dark And Grim
01.08.2004

Many different things … *changed my life.*

I was born in Belgrade but I grew up in Lagos. I also lived a bit in Missouri and Paris and a bit more in Milano. I don't know what else to say about myself: there is so much, yet none of it seems important.

www.tosic.com

I organized a small meeting of people while I was still losing weight, and we played with a camera and me: I was wearing underwear, a cowboy hat and boxing gloves and was making retarded faces. Turned out it was great fun and when Sebastian, through Rafael, invited me to produce a piece for this magazine I was happy to explore this a bit more.

01

02

04

03

05

01, 02
Nakitu Minayashi
You may buy this book of poetry I wrote from www.nakituminayashi.com or www.cascoprojects.org

03
Cyberkebab
A poster distributed through the walls of Nantes

04
My Second Film
The film itself is not so interesting but I like the text I did for it

05
Document Photos
Several years of work so far, each time I need to get a government document I take a different strange photo for it. All these photos have been accepted in my documents including my current passport. Check www.tosic.com/document_photos for more info

Steven Preston

154
Untitled

[see also: Graphic 01, pp172-173]

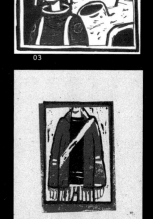

Black ink … *changed my life.*

Steven Preston was born in Norwich and has lived in London and Berlin. He has drawn comic-strips; ranging in subject matter from the loneliness of space travel to Ulrike Meinhof. None of his comics are funny. In fact, some of them are downright sad. He has had work printed in England and Germany and is also designer for Typocrat Press; a small-press publisher dedicated to publishing English-language versions of the best new European cartoonists.

stevenjpreston@hotmail.com
steven@typocrat.com
www.typopcrat.com

01

02

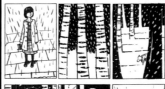

04

05

01
Promotional illustration for
Wolfen clothing label
Berlin, 2004

02
From untitled word-less comic strip
for Wolfen clothing label
Berlin, 2004

03
Sketch for splash page for work-in-progress Sputnik strip

04
From untitled, wordless comic strip
for Wolfen clothing label
Berlin, 2004

03
Self-Promotion
two colour woodblock print postcard
2003

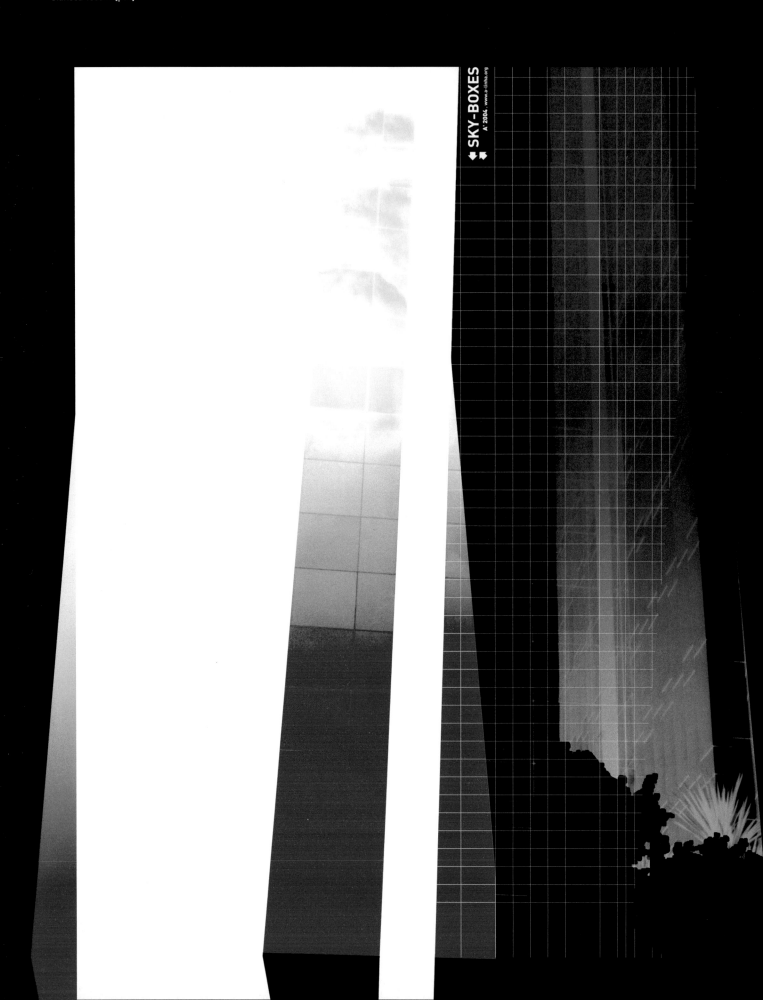

OVERTHROW A PART OF YOURSELF,

POCKETS BELTS SKIRT

chez Fred

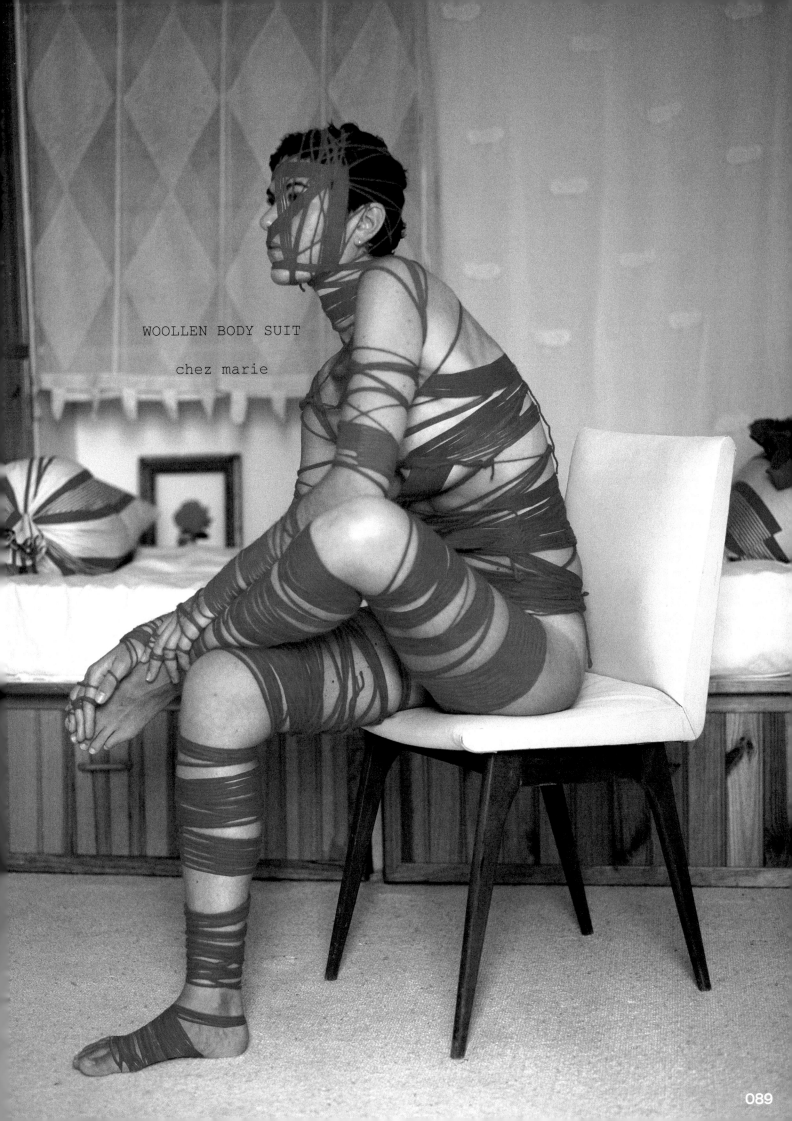

WOOLLEN BODY SUIT

chez marie

OUTLINE DRESS

chez Justin

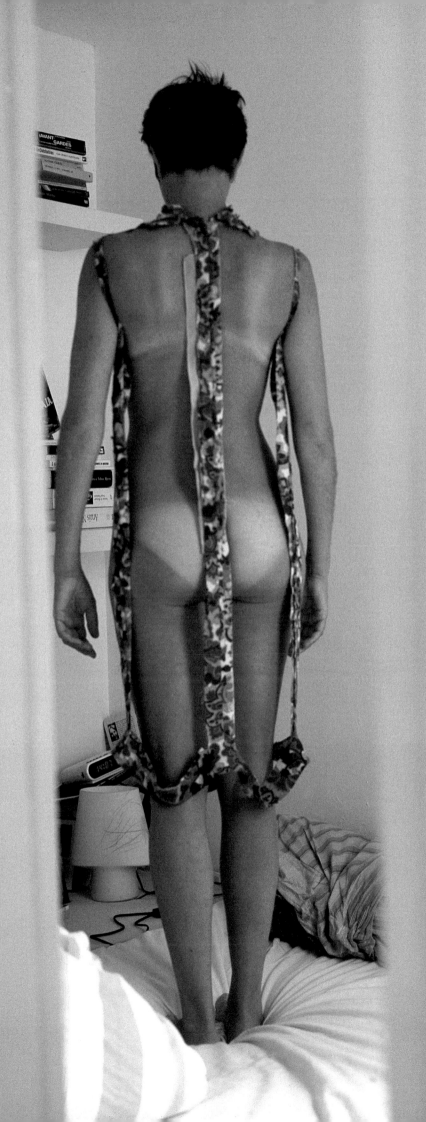

FOUR SLEEVES OR 2ARMS&1SCARF

chez Mario

Making Rain Serve the People

For thousands of years, people have been at the mercy of the rain. Rain casts a shadow over our working lives, destroys recreational interludes and decimates great pinnacles of man-made ingenuity.

Over a period of 20 years, the Precipitation Investigative Committee has conducted studies on rain behavior: regimentation, infiltration, saturation and other established soaking and battery strategies, seeking once and for all to eliminate the pluvial problem.

A myriad of conclusions have been drawn on the devious and dissembling nature of rainfall, which, for reasons of space, cannot be addressed here. Rather, we recommend a short revolutionary manifesto available to order from the P.I.C. Headquarters, for inclusion in school textbooks, leaflets and other relevant instructional publications.

Mobilize Futility! Say No To Bad Weather!

Less Rain Anthem

Stand up, oh sodden ones
Rise, and let the newly shining sun
Dry your clothes and your tears
For the day of eternal blue sky undoubtedly nears.

Children laugh
And ancients weep
To see the old rain
Sink in earth so deep
Evaporate and rise again, it may,
But fall again – never! – we'll find a way.

The rainbow brings glad tides of joy
Victory, vanquishment, like a child's new toy
Lie bathed in sunshine
On sweet-meadow plains.

Rise up, oh weary wet
Stand tall, children of Apollo
For those dark and ominous clouds
With their swollen bellies of menace
Will pass, and we can all play tennis!

NOT THE YELLOW BRICK ROAD

Zarafshan, of which I am showing several impressions, is the hub of the Uzbek gold mining industry, a surviving soviet dream, a version of Tim Burton's vision of suburbia. Life as a cog in well-oiled utopia, metallic efficiency in weird harmony with the dumbly sentimental cycle of euphoria and submission, vodka and hangovers. Outdoor restaurants with a hundred coloured plastic chairs, brown-sweet flavour ice cream in government-issue cast crystal bowls. On this mild evening beneath the silent treetops, miners mingle with Mafiosi. They giggle and eye up the graceful single mothers walking their toddlers along the promenade, lined with loudspeakers on lampposts, oozing watery Russian pop. A table of smug and cagey guys from Arizona,massive arms crossed, bored of the pork shashlik, but the money's ok, they say, as the murals behind them fade up along the towerblock walls in the twilight. The fairground nearby is defunct. Loitering by the crumbling waltzer, all doomed innocence, are the kids, their heads full of adventures. The local football team is playing Samarkandt this Sunday at the stadium just off the central square, entry free. If they've let you into Zarafshan to start with, that is. Two hundred miles of desert radius, two roads in, blocked by heavily fortified, looming checkpoints over-staffed with cops, who are not shy.

Throughout this big, flat country, a sense of dead calm permeates every thing like chalky dust. Might it be somehow comforting to live immobilized, pushed right up against a tightly drawn line you cross only at your peril? We meet the bravest people, little people. Pilawov and his wife grow tomatoes, cucumbers, cherries on two little plots on the very edge of Zafarabad, a mile and a half from the first uranium leaching site, to feed themselves and their disabled son. They radiate the rare warmth of tears dried up, have paused in that lucid state of numbness and tolerance, as they invite us in to share their bread and oil and story. They built themselves a shack here, illegally, and he fixes stuff for people, buckets, roofs, exhausts. You can't move or work anywhere without a permit. A permit is expensive. Before this he was in jail for ten years, completely cut off. During that time, his two brothers died in mining accidents. His home village is now a ghost town, not far away, where his daughter is he doesn't know. Maybe only pointless courage can soothe the restless soul.

The oppressive apparatus is extensive, well funded, and arbitrarily ultra-violent to just that finely tuned degree that induces the maximum sustainable level of fear in the population. Anyone suspected of dissent may be arrested on charges ranging from 'subversion' and 'homosexuality' to being 'too pious'. That and the odd planting in chosen flats or pockets of that little lump of opium. Torture is a routine procedure and has lately culminated in several cases of prisoners being boiled alive. Craig Murray, the heroically outspoken British ambassador to Tashkent, now dragged into a muddy legal battle with the Home Office, describes the Uzbek regime as 'kleptocratic'.

There will probably, by most foreign observer's accounts, be violent political change in Uzbekistan soon. Now you can see it coming, a cloud of dust on the far horizon, and now you can't, a hairline crack in the lid of a pressure cooker. It's going to be messy, out of a stealthy nowhere like a rusty rocket-propelled grenade, bloody and inarticulate, still, for most, better than the present state.

Ernst Fischer, 2004

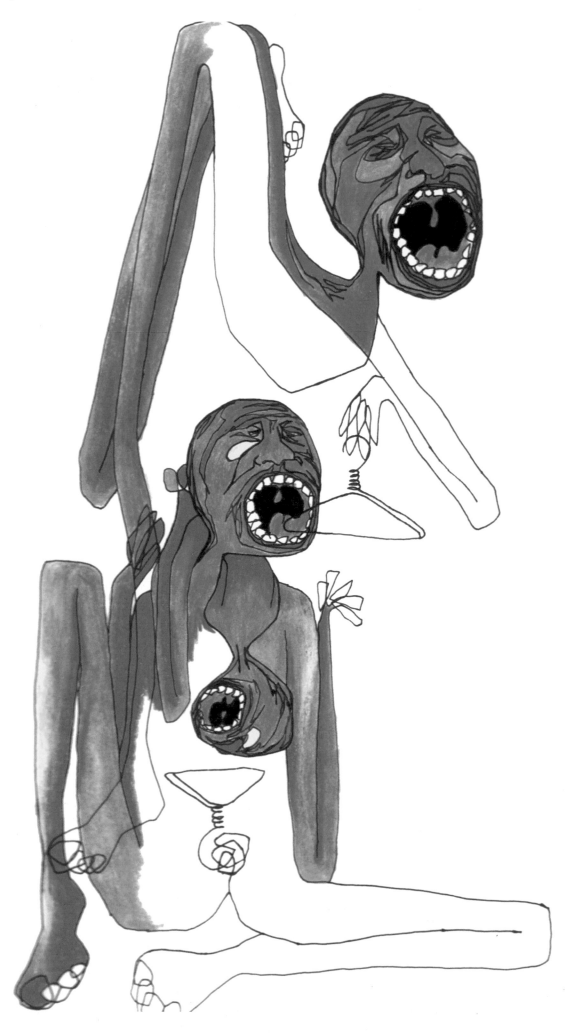

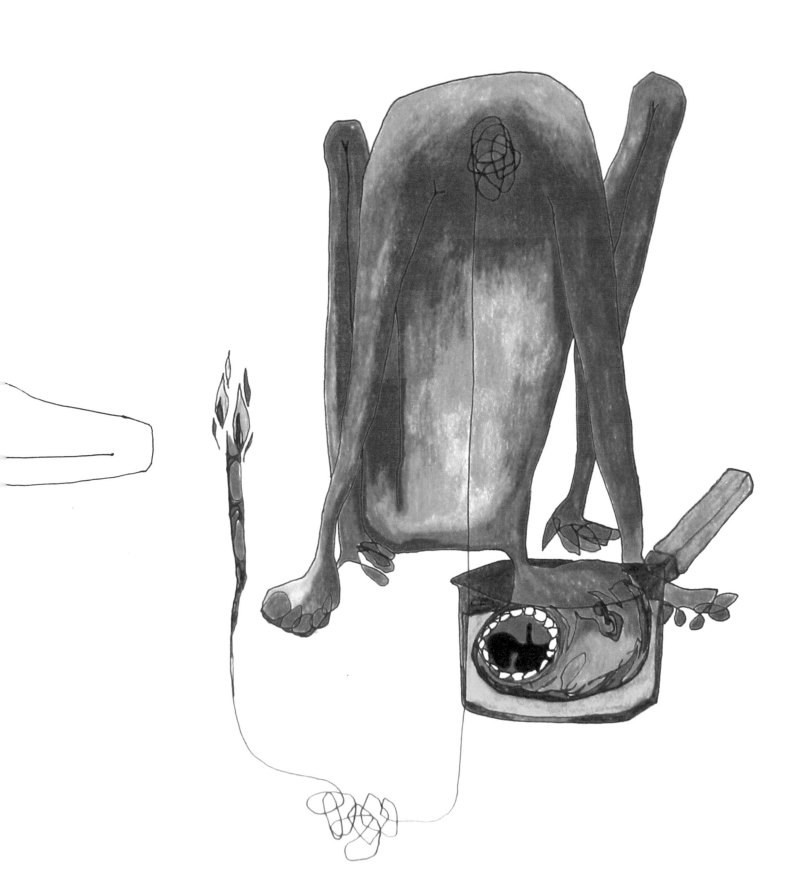

üse

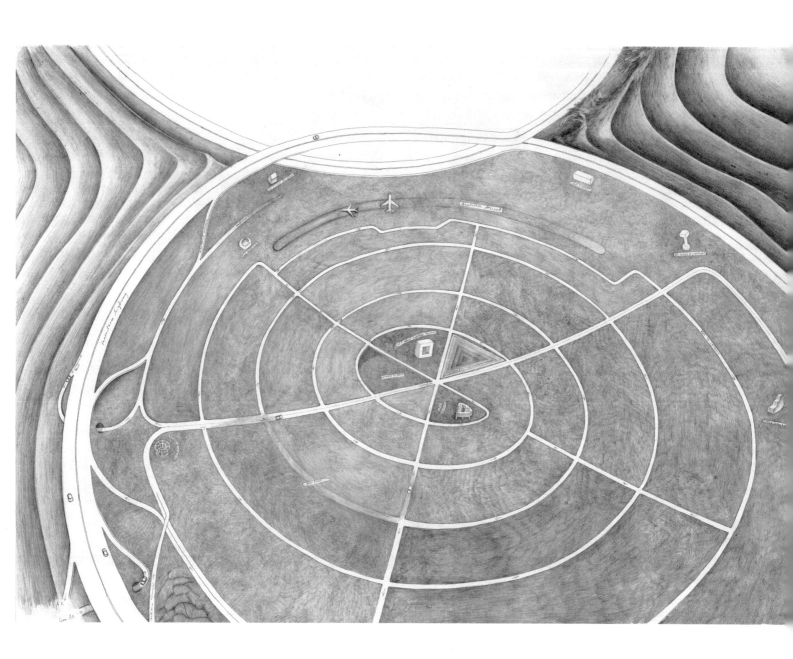

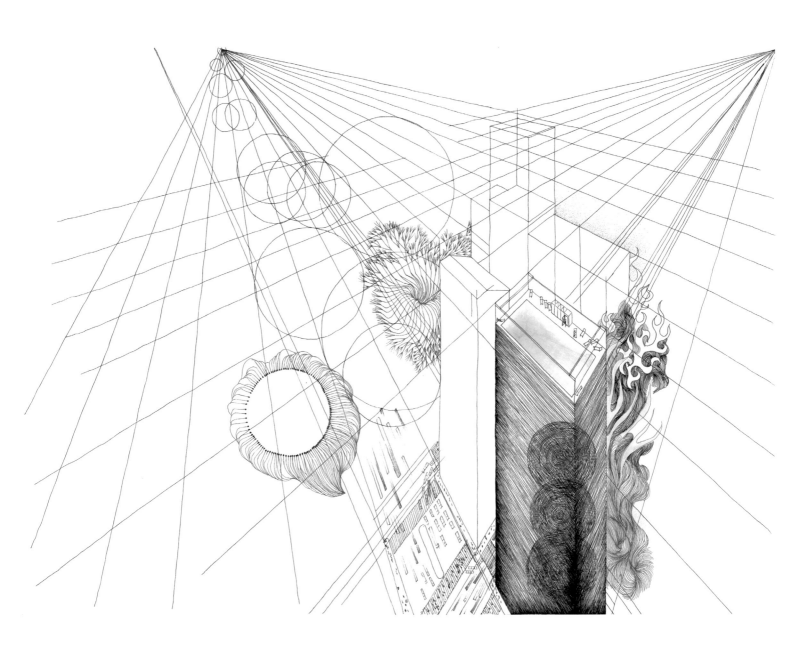

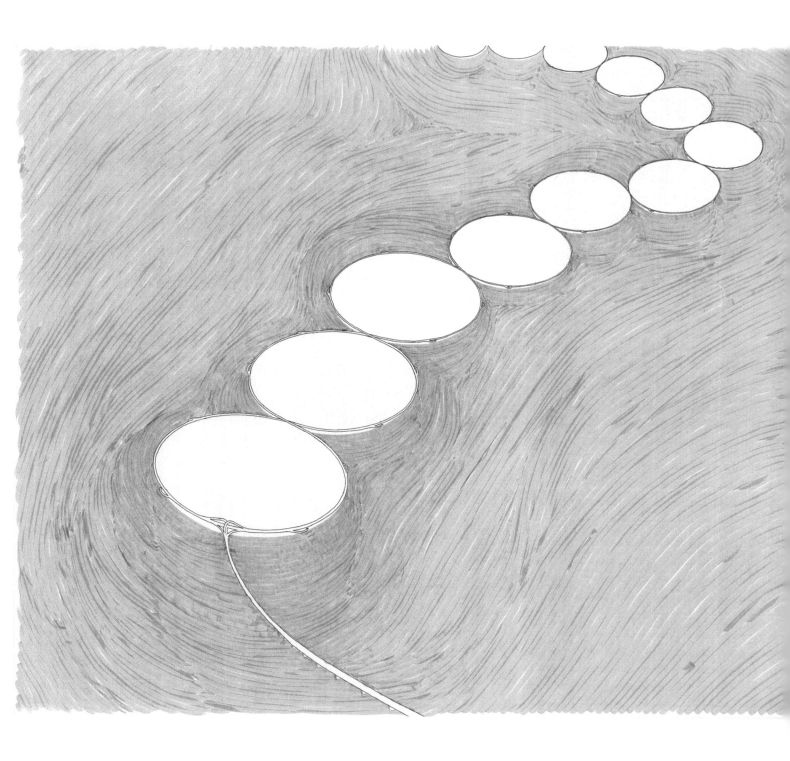

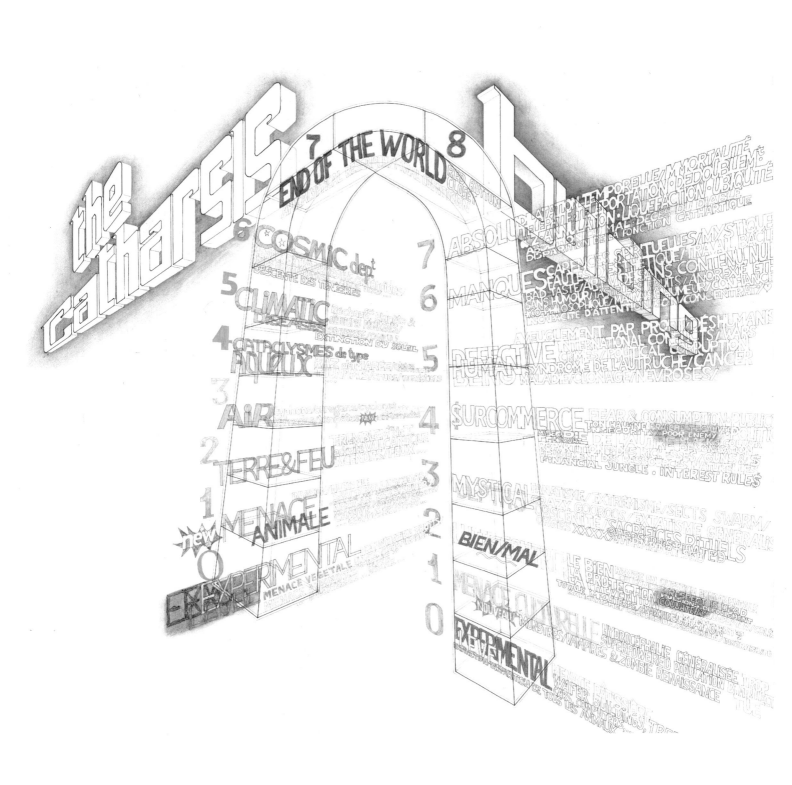

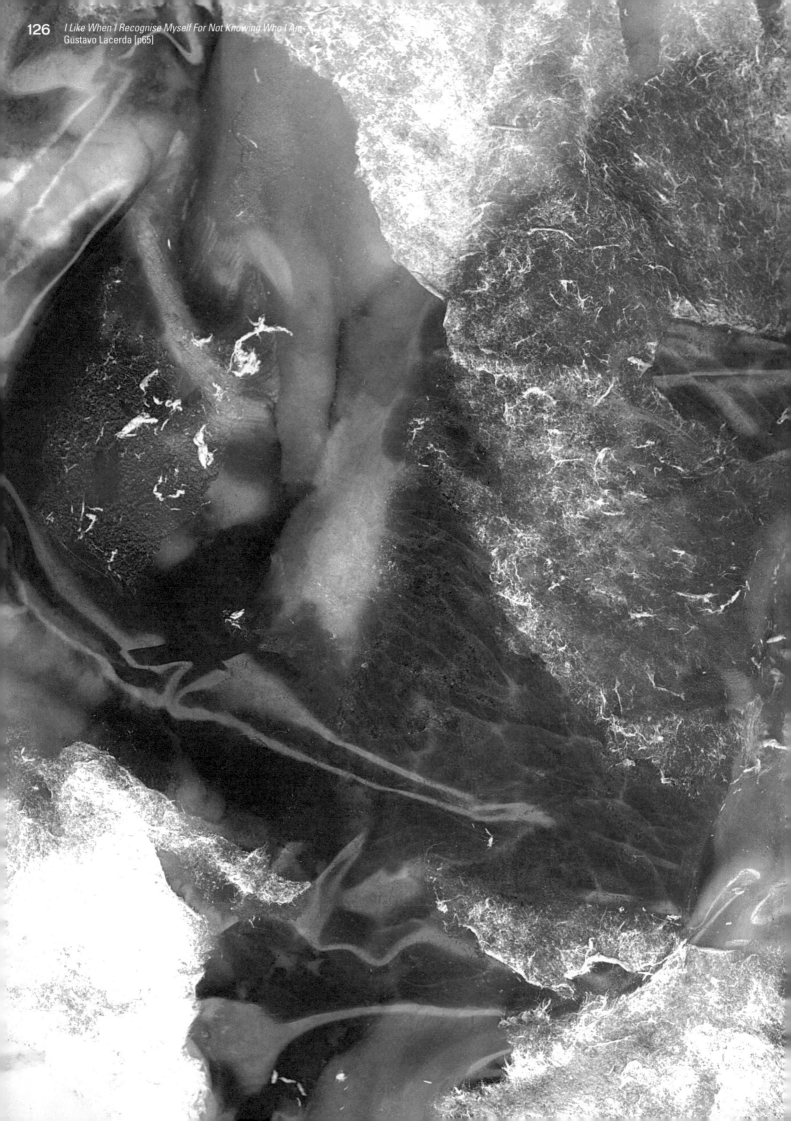

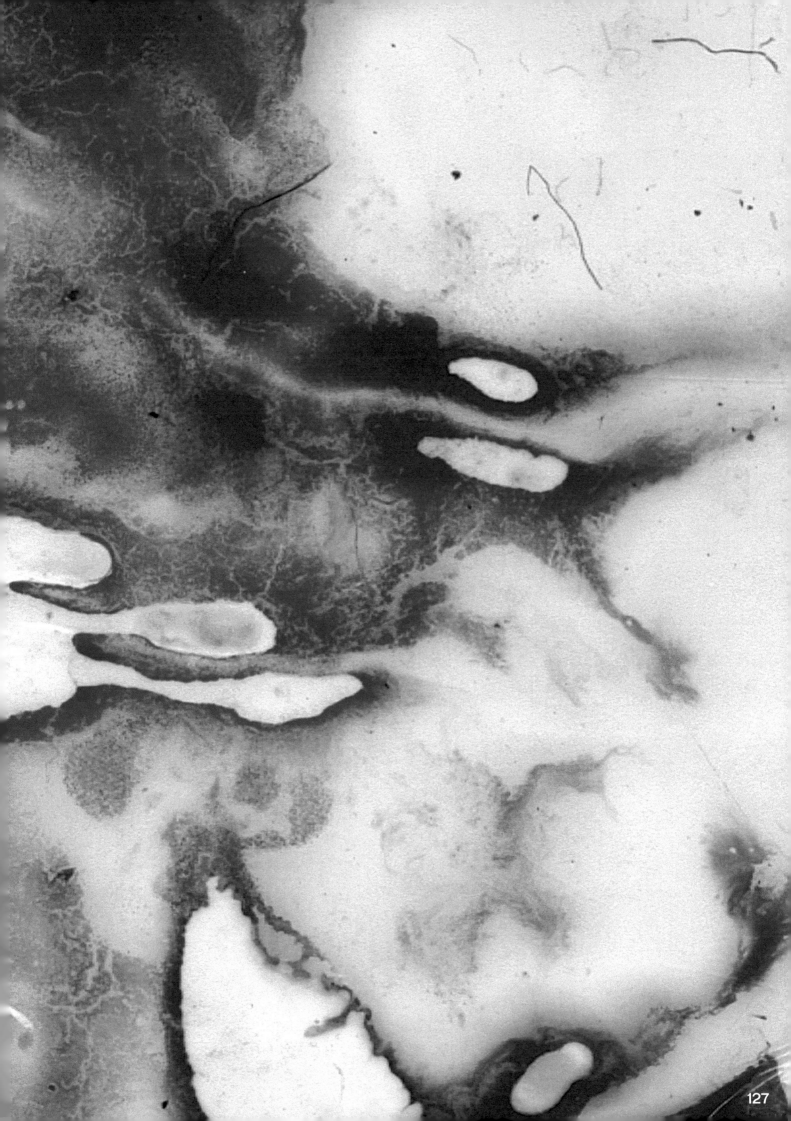

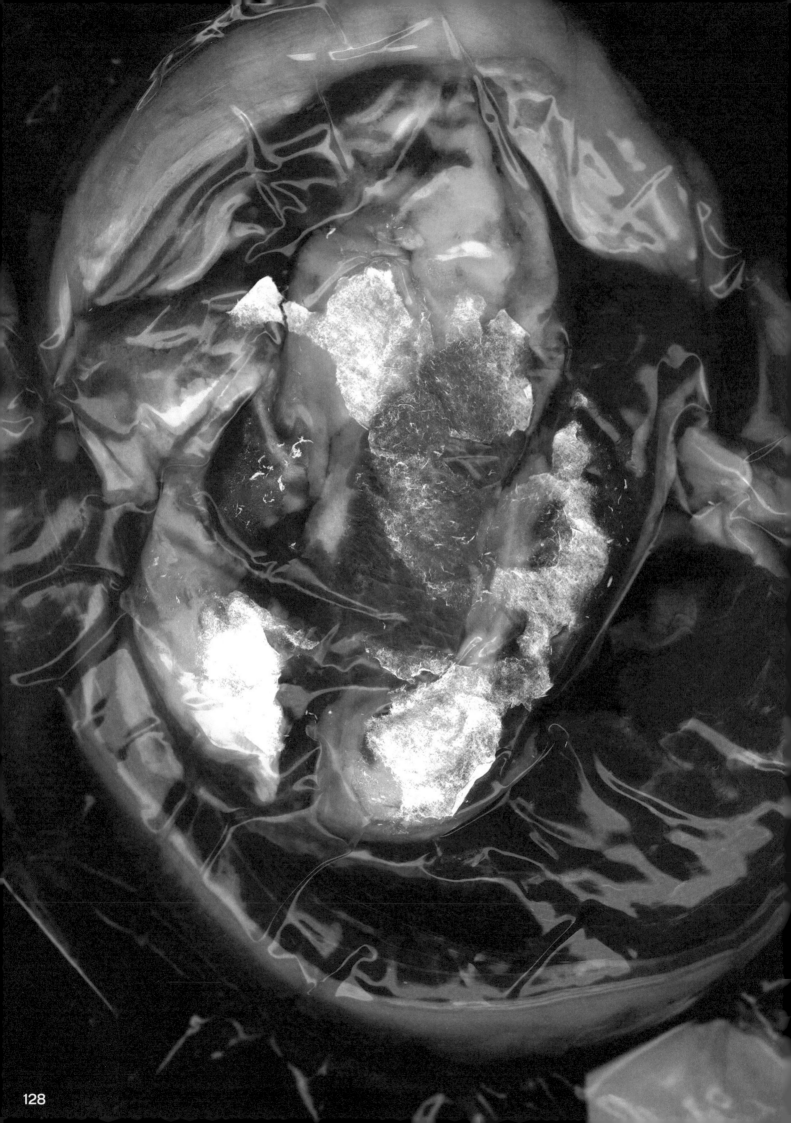

I LIKE WHEN I RECOGNISE MYSELF
FOR NOT KNOWING WHO I AM

Untitled
Niko Stumpo [p65]

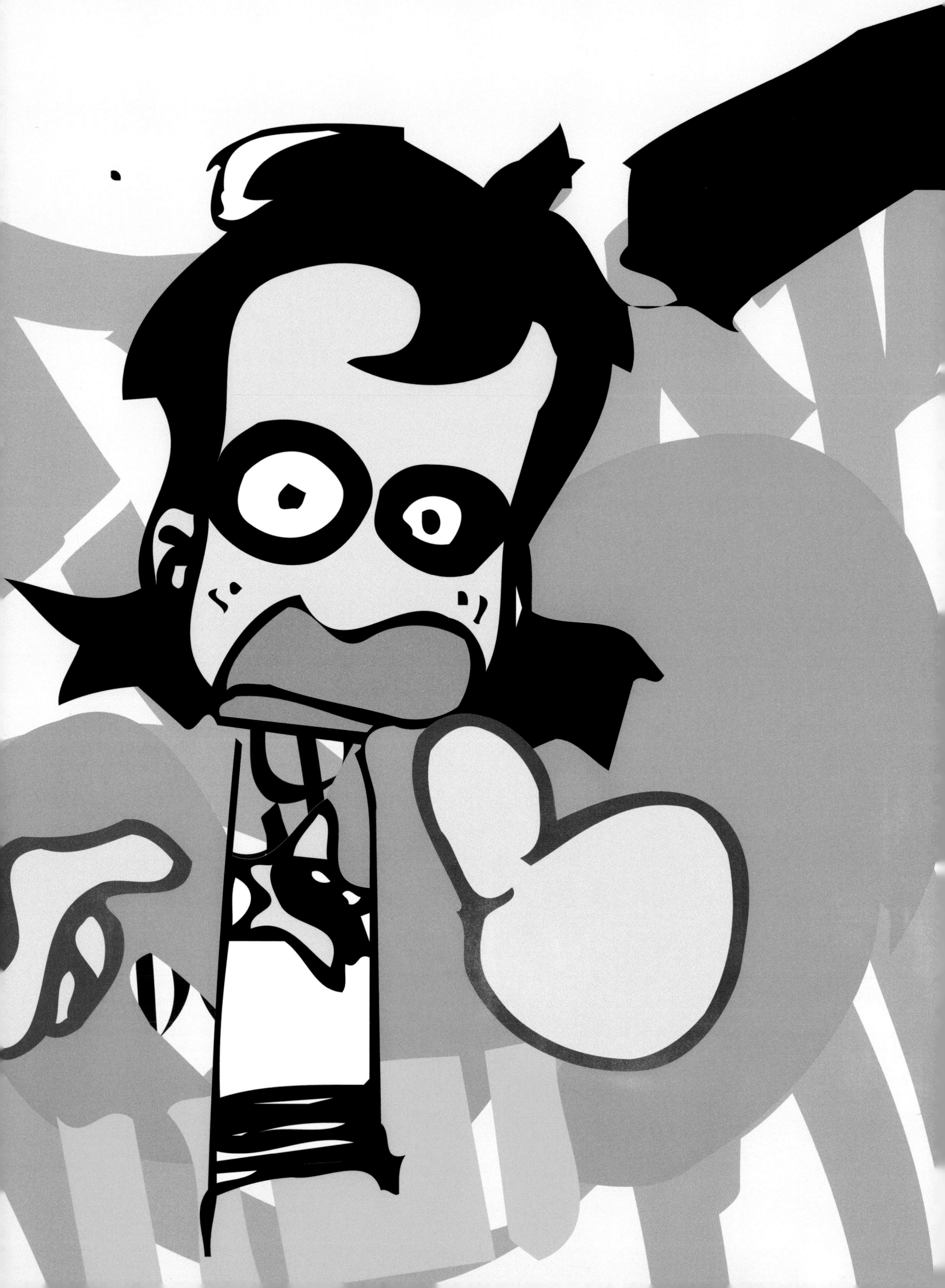

THE BED REVOLUTION MANIFESTO

People die in beds. In fact you'll probably die in a bed. John Lennon died on a street but he did try to start a revolution from his bed. The anagram of 'a bed' is ALMOST 'dead'. Do you think that they're trying to tell us something?

84% of
people die
in a bed,
throw it out
live forever

GET RID OF
YOUR BED BEFORE
IT RIDDENS YOU

YOU'VE MADE
YOUR BED
NOW DIE IN IT

84% of people die in a bed, throw it out, live forever,

MONSTERS
SCHMONSTERS

84% of people die in a bed,
throw it out, live forever,

THE FUTURE IS DARK AND GRIM

———

This future is neither too far
nor too close. Vast devastation
occurred which dried the oceans and
made the planet look like a bigass
desert full of very tall mountains.
Old civilizations do not exist and new
people live in strange new societies
full of strange new religions. They
all still dream of the seas which they
never saw.

SOLDIER

Has a brain controller which makes him stupid all the time so he
does not question the chain of command, has superdooperultradeath
gloves which are the best weapons around and most importantly
he wears many different colours which attract females so he can make lots
of new little soldiers.

TEACHER

Always a female because men have better things to do. Teachers never
walk on rough terrain so they can allow themselves to wear pretty soft
shoes. Also has an arm band which glows in hypnotical colours so students
of all ages can shut up and listen. Scarf has no purpose because
in the future it is never below 50°C. Red belt means this teacher works
only with 60 year olds and probably teaches paperwork and how to forget
the fear of death.

COOK

Cooks or 'the ones that make and prepare food' are the most powerful
and influential group in the new society – or at least they like to think so.
It is sure they are very arrogant so most other groups created
The SCCG (The Secret Cook Control Group) which lobbied with
the new bureaucrats that enforced the law that made all cooks
wear small black device around their chest. Cooks are told this makes their
penises bigger but what it actually does is make them more afraid
of authority.

PLAYBOY

There is no concept of money in this future, only the concept of power. Hence the definition of a playboy is different, he or she is the one who does nothing or does only things which kill time through fun. He also has soft shoes and nice wide pillow pants which on a touch of a button turn into a bed so he can sleep whenever and wherever he wants. The usual sleep/not sleep schedule which applies to other 99,99999 % of the population is not followed by playboys (or playgirls). The dark smelly cloth over the face is the latest fashion.

HOUSEWOMAN

Wears many colors which help her procreate and she also has a very
necessary brain control device which makes her stupid yet great at sex.
They are told this is jewelry so they love it. They are always home and they
often sit while they look over the house, pets and the children so they have
open foot shoes and advanced sitting wear. Thanks to new discoveries
in future medicine housewomen can bear 27 children each year until they
turn 50 and they also are very sexy until 50 because they need to attract
so much procreation.

BUREAUCRAT

Why a bureaucrat also has a pair of superdooperultradeath gloves
is very clear in the future – because he needs to engage in deadly
confrontations on a daily basis and a private army is not an option.
His jacket is also a life saver because it can successfully defend him
from great heat, a riot, a 10 kilometer fall, a shark attack, all kinds
of viruses and a nuclear blast.

PARTY GIRL

Party girl is not like Playboy. Playboy spends money while Party Girl makes money. It is not really clear which is in a better position because playboys must impress and spend money to have sex while for party girls it is enough to exist and someone comes over and offers them money to have sex with them. Future in the dry oceans obviously favors women in this case.

everything is dark

and there are no walls

the forest is full of ghosts

but the machine never sleeps

inside, everything is electrified

lonely..

longing..

the powerstation is silent

writing with jolts of pain

and unrestrained joy

alive

alive

alive

endlessly spinning and swinging

this house should have been
set in the heavens
so the gods could live in it

instead it is a fallen cathedral

a warehouse filled with junk

all scrap iron and faulty electronics

everything is dark..

Have you heard of the term VJ? Maybe? But what exactly do they do? Most of us know that they're involved with projections in nightclubs and bars, but where did they come from and what's the future of VJing?

The Future of VJing

Text by Karl Sadler

There are probably many different stories about where VJing was spawned from, but generally the material used in early video projection emerged from the rave scene. The low budget, abstract fractal and psychedelic effects created on computers, which mirrored the lighting effects and lasers in clubs at the time, later evolved into video performance. Some 90's dance music videos aimed at MTV, borrowed some of the effects used in this early form of VJing to add a 'club feel' to the videos.

VJing has developed since then, and many VJs have backgrounds in design, film and broadcast as well as an understanding of lighting which bring different elements of creativity to the field. After the dot-com boom a few years ago, many ex-web designers are also now also tackling VJing.

A VJ playing a set in a venue will typically mix or manipulate video, whether it be their own material or found footage, whilst a DJ or live band take care of the music. In some cases a VJ set is prepared like an installation with edited video-footage, to be played back on multiple screens or with a combination of both live mixing and prepared work.

Recently, the rise of new digital visual arts, cheaper technology and more readily available software such as Motion Dive and Vjamm, which allow anyone to perform visuals simply with a laptop computer and a video projector, has flooded the VJ scene with inexperienced artists prepared to work for very little, creating a threat to existing VJs. Specialist expensive hardware is no longer needed. This has made VJs realise that simply working as a club VJ no longer pays the bills. This has been an incentive for professional VJs to push the art form away from nightclubs into different mediums and formats like TV, galleries and producing their own custom software.

Addictive TV is an interesting collective of VJs and DJs who I met through DJ magazine. Addictive TV grabbed my attention, not only because they are cutting edge professional VJs, but I discovered they were behind the production and concept for a television program called Mixmasters on ITV. The program showcases contemporary electronic music and video in the form of audiovisual streams of mixed together work. They also run a DVD label releasing the AV works featured in the series.

I met with Graham Daniels from Addictive TV to ask him about the future of VJing, and certain issues which are not usually touched upon. I began by asking Graham how he saw VJing progressing in the near future?

GD: VJs have to come out of clubs. When today's electronic music culture came about there was an infrastructure already in place for it, like nightclubs and radio, venues for what we're doing don't quite exist. Obviously there's television, but we're the only people in the UK doing it on TV. There needs to be more people doing it on television, even cable stations, like after midnight, video streams of live visual remixing, VJing and Djing.

KS: How do you think VJs can personally develop?

GD: If VJing remains only as a live medium, only servicing the audio industry and only performing in clubs, there is no future in that. It's a sad way perspective, to think that this is the only way it can be done. VJs have to become visual recording artists, they have to start creating their own work, they have to start getting out there, either working closely with audio artists and collaborating to release DVDs, or you know, making music themselves. Audio Visual is the future, AV acts performing. I think that's the way forward. I thought that without VJs performing in nightclubs, club promoters would purchase DVDs such as Onedotzero's and Gas' with the intention of playing them as visuals at club nights, using these DVDs as an alternative to employing a VJ.

New technology is going to make the mixing of visuals easier and more fun, but the challenge remains the same - to create compelling content and present it in exciting formats

KS: What's your opinion on this?

GD: If you're not going to pay for visuals, then promoters shouldn't be playing some of the best visuals around - visuals that artists have spent months toiling over in order to release on DVD for people to buy and watch at home. There is a PRS (Performing Rights Society) system in clubs that supports the audio artists rights to play their work and, even though a lot of clubs don't adhere to it, there is a structure in place. Music in clubs is different to visuals. You want DJs to play your music

in a club, because if it becomes a hit you can license the music to compilation albums, and what you really want to do is get radio play, and as soon as it's on radio you're picking up PRS and royalties. With visuals none of that exists, a punter won't see some great visuals, and somehow, get broadcast on television as a result of crowd reaction and receive any kind of royalties. The structures that exist between moving image and music are very different.

I would tend to agree with Graham. The structure is not there yet. Digital art and motion graphics are supported by film festivals like RES, Onedotzero and Antenna. These festivals are successful in showcasing the latest cutting edge music videos and shorts, but there isn't as yet and event focussing on VJs, an event which could possibly discover the latest underground talent. I asked Giles Thacker, a professional VJ and ex-video artist for Orbital's live shows, how he saw the VJ's role developing over the next few years?

GT: More live acts, maybe even one that gets mainstream recognition, and less interest in traditional nightclub VJing. New technology is going to make the mixing of visuals easier and more fun, but the challenge remains the same - to create compelling content and present it in exciting formats.

Is VJing in need of something more entrancing? Something other than a crude-looking music video or hyper edited holiday footage? I personally find the majority of VJs' material difficult to pallet. There's this argument focusing on the need for VJing material to move beyond the nightclub. But this is tricky. The very nature of visuals created for clubs means that they have no narrative or story, which makes it difficult for anyone to see the video as anything other than something that looks pretty. It's generally not conceptual, not intellectual. The typical visuals used in VJing work in the 90s dance music scene, but that era has now been and gone. It's already dated,

just like iMovie's built-in transitions and wipes, this stuff is cheesy.

AV acts (an AV artist controls both the music and the visuals) are the way forward, bands or electronic musicians incorporating visuals into their performances. This isn't to say that projecting exciting irrelevant flashing animation behind laptop musicians won't make them look any more interesting. I think stage performances with bands could be enhanced with projections, but if they were thought out almost as a form of virtual set design, where landscapes could move and characters interact with the musician. The band Gorillaz performed in a similar way, but it would be clever if these animations could be controlled live, almost like controlling a computer game. Because isn't that supposed to be one of the important elements of VJing - live manipulation?

The future of VJing is obviously in the rise of more VJs. Laptops are now more affordable and we'll be getting VJ software free with our breakfast cereal next. But does that mean we'll still be watching people video-mixing their home videos with those kaleidoscope effects and looping their dog barking repetitively, or will new talent break into the limelight?

A bit of a catch-22. There needs to be an alternative platform for someone to perform as a VJ, something other than the nightclub, but there also needs to be a better quality of work to make it worthwhile.

*   *   *

Karl Sadler is Format.K, a Music Producer, Animator, and VJ who collaborates with Spam under the name The Kitchen Staff, and is part of the collective Werk (v-urk), which runs various club nights as well as being a record label.

www.werk-it.com/thekitchenstaff/

Only videogames could bring you a rampage of theft and destruction which will melt your heart.

01
The sleeve art for Katamari Damacy perfectly illustrates Namco's understanding of creating emotion through aesthetics rather than narrative.
Artwork © Namco Ltd. 2003

DRINKING GAMES

Text by Margaret Robertson

The King of Space is drunk. So drunk that his swoops and staggers have smashed the stars and darkened the skies. Sobered, he calls upon you to collect the raw material to birth new stars and you, of course, agree.

As stories go, it could hardly be any more scant. It wouldn't fill a feature film, or a book whose pages weren't made out of cardboard. Videogames, however, have always thrived on similarly pithy, deranged set-ups. And this one, which forms the backdrop to Namco's Katamari Damacy, couldn't be any more densely, dreamily delightful. The logic may be loony, but there's an irresistible inevitability to it, one that it would be churlish to refuse. The King of Space is drunk and you, of course, agree.

However, it's one thing to make a pledge to a cosmic king who's tied one on. It's another to deliver. Just what have you got yourself into? Another few hours of repetitive sofa time? Shooting things and collecting tokens? Or jumping on things and collecting tokens? Not this time. Instead, find a fat ball of blu-tak and warm it in your fingers. Smooth it to a round and let it loose on your desk. Roll it while it picks up paper clips, pen tops, matches and Smarties - a spare key, perhaps, or a watch battery. And that's it. End of your mild, absent-minded fun. Nothing to write an article about, that's for sure.

This, however, is where videogames come in. They are at their strongest not when they offer an extension of the obvious ('I wish I could drive a teensy bit faster and then win Wimbledon!') but when they allow an elaboration of something we'd barely considered. In Katamari, your blu-tak ball never stops growing, never loses its stick. Each new objects glues itself to the last: keys beget socks beget books beget cushions beget chairs beget doors, paving stones, fences, buses and bungalows, lakes and lay-bys, planes and rainbows. From tiny, sticky acorns do giant stars-in-waiting grow.

This is a game of incremental kleptomania. Everything you can see, you can have. But not yet, never quite yet. A small ball can only pick up small things. But these small things make your ball bigger, and a bigger ball can pick up bigger things. Each time you circle the pastel plainness of a Japanese suburb you log the items you will poach on your next lap. As they attach, each item blooms into life. Eggs hatch, dogs bark,

people sing shrill, panicky songs. Your ball becomes a gleeful cacophony of butterflies and geese, lollipops and handcuffs, studded with Elvis quiffs and telegraph poles.

The first time you realise that Katamari is something truly special is when you introduce it to a friend and watch it reduce them to childishness. This, usually, is a bad thing. Childish has become synonymous with moronic, clumsy, sentimental and boring, all the traits in which bad games usually excel. It's singularly unfair. The rapid learning and the eagerness for exploration and experiment that children exhibit are exactly the tendencies which good videogames encourage from the second you switch them on. Watching an adult undergo the child's learning process that Katamari demands is both touching and unsettling. It's a game that generates its own litany, identical regardless of the person who is playing. First cautious: 'Can you pick up flowers?' 'You can pick up everything.' Then curious: 'Can you pick up the people?' 'You can pick up everything.' Then sceptical: 'Can you pick up cars?' 'You can pick up everything,' Then calculating: 'Can you pick up islands?' 'You can pick up everything.' Finally understanding: 'Can you pick … oh. You can pick up *everything*.'

This alone would set Katamari apart, guarantee it a place on the reading list for What Games Do That Nothing Else Can. But as you play, a darker, clever core is revealed. In Katamari you start out small. Cotton reels and rubbers thump into you like bumper cars. A squealing mouse looms like a predator. Trundling round the skirting boards and gutters you feel half like a pint-pot hero, half like a virtuous recycler. But as you go, you grow. And as you grow you become the predator. The people whose shoes you once couldn't see over start to scream as you approach. Police fire useless shots at your thundering bulk. You amass first their children and then their cars, their livelihoods and then their houses. A thriving town becomes as bare as a car lot, a rich green forest as scoured as a desert. Your actions become steadily more violent. Wrenching islands free of their sockets feels as sickening as a slowly pulled tooth. In the end, you're a monster, a real life Shiva.

A thousand sci-fi novels have painted the death of worlds devoured by a hungry star as it flares outward and engulfs a galaxy. Katamari shows you an insidious alternative: worlds devoured by a star that timidly nibbles from the inside out. It's a cosmic version of the fate of the unfortunate Jim, who, courtesy of a nibbling lion, finds out 'how it feels, when first your toes and then your heels, and then by gradual degrees your shins and ankles, calves and knees are slowly eaten bit by bit'. While Jim may have detested it, you will relish every second. Those seconds, however, will have an emotional

Katamari is like taking a child that's lived on cheese that comes out of a tube and stuffing a perfect tomato into their mouth: a time bomb of bitter nourishment and sweet, scented savour

richness which games that profess 'deep' stories and 'cinematic' sequences are entirely unable to provoke. Katamari is a game which forces you to respond to what you do, not what you're told. Katamari is a game which uses its form, rather than fighting it.

Katamari Damacy is not yet confirmed for a release in Europe. Conventional, and somewhat racist, wisdom is that this kind of Japanese 'wackiness' is too rich for our thin Northern blood. They're right, in a way. The thick, useless mulch of most of today's videogames is a pretty poor diet. Katamari is like taking a child that's lived on cheese that comes out of a tube and stuffing a perfect tomato into their mouth: a time bomb of bitter nourishment and sweet, scented savour. Frightening, extraordinary and actually wonderful. Isn't that the least we deserve?

*　*　*

Margaret Robertson is Games Editor of Edge magazine.
www.edge-online.com
www.katamaridamacy.jp

Goody two-shoes have become the biggest rebels on the block, and this mood has, in turn, had an inevitable effect on designers.

Hip to be square

Text by Rosanna Vitiello

I am by no means a rebel. When I was nineteen, prime time for teenage rebellion, I remember my father telling me I was too conformist. I don't smoke, I don't do drugs, I don't drink much; I don't really indulge in any of those stereotypical marks of rebellion. I'm often described as 'sensible,' Bizarrely, I've been told I have the face of a saint, and when I was a child, my friends (incorrectly) thought I never lied. So no, I may seem boring, but I am by no means a rebel.

But where are the real rebels nowadays? How many rebels do you know anyway? In Western society at least, we're exposed to so much through both the media and everyday life, that we've become increasingly harder to offend. Traditional acts of rebellion (if such a term can exist) of sex, drugs and rock 'n' roll just don't have the same shock factor they once did. This summer's Big Brother was more like a peep show than a reality show, but that is the reality today. If every morning across Britain we can enjoy our cereal over a pair of page three breasts, it becomes easy to forget that these were once considered scandalous, especially in a country that is traditionally shy and conservative when it comes to naked bodies.

Drugs are part of the social landscape too. Acquiring a smack habit will never be considered a great career move, but class A drugs don't hold the same taboo they once might have. When Blue Peter presenter Richard Bacon got caught out on a coke binge, it kick started his TV career. He wasn't considered cringingly innocent anymore; he was accepted into the normal world as one of us. With 76% of 23 year olds in the UK having taken drugs, and more than half remaining active, it's those who abstain who are considered the odd ones out.

And Rock 'n' Roll? Well, we've never really lived in the times of 'Footloose', that cult 80s film where dancing was banned from small town America. But, when punk king Johnny Rotten appears on "I'm a celebrity get me out of here,' I think that says it all.

Even tattoos don't count as markers of rebellion anymore. Once confined to criminals and sailors, we now see clean-cut celebrities like Beckham covered in them. They just don't have that unacceptable edge they once did, partly because the majority tattoos you now see depict a dolphin peeking out of the top of girls' hipsters. And we've all got piercings. A ten-year old recently asked me if I had my belly button pierced. When I said 'No,' she replied puzzled, 'Why not?' The widespread nature of all of these symbolic acts of rebellion means that their potency has become highly diluted. So if what was once considered extreme is now much more acceptable, what's left to protest against?

This poses a bit of a problem for anyone who considers themselves 'creative'. If rebellion is all about thinking differently, going against what's accepted, then creativity, in it's own way, is a form of rebellion. Creative people don't like to think of themselves as doing what they're told, and whether rebels are creative or creative minds are rebellious, it works both ways.

So what is the designer's role in rebellion? In the past, design rebels have fed off the anger and excitement they saw in society around them. It's no accident that the Italian 'Radical' or 'Anti-Design' movement coincided with a wave of political revolt across Europe in the late 1960s. The Parisian student riots in 1968 and a spate of terrorist bombings across Italy, created political debate and confusion. Such upheaval established a mindset of change in Italy, which fed directly into the anti-design movement. As a direct challenge to the modernist orthodoxy, anti-design's post-modern attitude rejected pure function, instead opting for a new, playful aesthetic. Architecture groups such as *Superstudio* and *Archizoom* promoted avant-garde, and initially utopian designs, such as *No-Stop City* and pure pleasure creations such as the *Superonda* chair. At the time, this was an approach and form of design that had never been seen before.

A decade later, Britain emerged as the focus of revolt. The situation in Northern Ireland, Thatcher, and trade union troubles all contributed to a climate that questioned the status quo. Drawing from this volatile atmosphere, Malcolm Maclaren, Vivienne Westwood and Jamie Reid, amongst others, heavily shaped the punk scene in England. Just as much as the music itself, punk is recognisable through its fashion and graphic statements. As Westwood said, 'You couldn't imagine the Punk Rock thing without the clothing.' Or without Jamie Reid's cut and paste album covers for the Sex Pistols. A born rebel, Westwood's attitude is pure revolutionary: 'The only reason I'm in fashion is to destroy the word conformity.'

That was then. But seeing as our source of rebellion's dried up, who's here to destroy conformity now? I was talking to a friend recently about the transformation of a girl she knew at St Martin's. We decided the college was akin to a stylistic conveyor belt; you go in sweet, innocent and a touch provincial. Then everyone gets the obligatory 'rebellious' haircut that makes your parents cringe (I had an undercut and an asymmetric fringe), and we all end up looking like we've got dressed in the dark. But a year or so after you've left, the effects wear off, and you look a little more acceptable to everyday society. It's not really rebellion, even if it looks that way to the outside world. But even the world at large is changing. Topshop has brought art student chic to the masses; Eley Kishimoto and Georgina Goodman now design for New Look. A couple of seasons ago it was all about 'customisation', even if that meant someone else had sewn patches onto your jacket for you. So if art school cool is just hi-

01
Borja Martinez
Pige-on (Restaurant)
Chalk on sidewalk
Barcelona 2004

'I am creating 'recreational areas'
for pigeons, (football pitches,
concentration camps, heliports,
courting areas, an oasis, etc...)Using
chalk I am able to interact with the
pigeons, and to offer them an epher-
ral environment, which is active and
dynamic. In this way I invite
the passer-by to reflect upon the
miserable state in which this urban
birds live.'
    Borja Martinez

street normal, we're back to our same old problem. What's left to rebel against?

The new breed of rebellion has gone full circle. It seems obvious; the only way to stick two fingers up to a fairly liberal establishment is to take what is commonly seen as a conformist stance. A devotion to religion, sexual abstention and teetotalism have become the new placards of protest. Goody two-shoes have become the biggest rebels on the block, and this mood has, in turn, had an inevitable effect on designers.

<u>Going back to the Punk movement</u>, the first thing we tend to associate with them is anarchy. But the ideals behind the Straight Edge punk movement turned the tables on the usual self-destruction and lawlessness. Borne out of Washington DC based Punk band, Minor Threat, in the early 80s, Straight Edgers take the basic philosophy of abstaining from anything they consider to be addictive or 'poisonous' to them. Ian MacKaye, the band's front man decided he didn't want to conform to what he saw around

him in the Punk scene. Why should he do drugs, get wasted and drunk just to fit it? In effect, MacKaye rejected the trends within his social circle, and in doing so created a new form of rebellion. He set out his feelings in a number of songs, such as 'Out of Step'. Lyrics such as 'Don't drink, Don't smoke, Don't fuck, At least I can fucking think' later came to be seen as a manifesto for the Straight Edge movement.

<u>MacKaye's lyrics promoted freedom of thought and the motivation to rebel against the crowd if the crowd isn't all it's cracked up to be</u>. But, as Straight Edge gathered ever more followers, McKay's ideals became tainted by a few who turned their back on the individual thought upon which the movement was founded. Straight Edgers started to get a reputation for violence against those who didn't adhere to their strict philosophy, attacking people who smoked or drank, as well as expelling members of their own group they caught out.

It seems obvious; the only way to stick two fingers up to a fairly liberal establishment is to take what is commonly seen as a conformist stance

Expulsion is almost a rite of passage for a rebel. And in October last year, Lila and Alma Lévy-Omari, two Muslim schoolgirls from a Paris suburb, joined that club. They were not kicked out of school for smoking, violence or drug dealing; none of the typical past times of a rebel. Rather they were expelled for wearing a headscarf. The French State, based heavily upon secular principles, decrees that whilst it is not illegal to wear religious symbols in schools, 'ostentatious' religious signs that 'constitute an act of pressure, provocation, proselytism or propaganda' are forbidden. The girls chose to wear a full headscarf, covering their ears, hairline and neck. The school considered this provocative, and threw them out.

In upholding their religious principles are Lila and Alma figureheads for a new breed of rebel? Their expulsion did act as a marker for a new social trend; Young European Muslims becoming increasingly devout, and rebelling against their more liberated parents. Nacira Guénif-Souilamas, a sociologist at the University of Paris XIII, has noted that girls are choosing to wear the headscarf younger, and are continuing to do so into adulthood. The trend is most marked among educated teenagers, whose exasperated mothers either never wore the veil, or actively fought to be liberated from it. Lila and Alma's mother is Algerian and doesn't wear a headscarf, whilst their father is Jewish.

In the same way that Straight Edgers have their black cross, and many Muslim women the headscarf, the symbol of virginity in the US is the silver ring. The Silver Ring Thing is just one of a growing number of sexual abstention movements in America, which have so far persuaded over 2.5 million young people to take a pledge of abstinence. Brought about as a backlash against what they see as the sexually liberated society promoted since the 60s, The Silver Ring Thing promotes its message through a travelling show, with sketches, flashy lighting, and above all, the silver ring which members wear until their wedding day. Denny Patteson, the movement's founder, describes their ideals as 'No sex before marriage, and that means no fooling around either.'

So what's the uptake of this new school of rebellion for designers? At first glance, design may be all about going against the current style to create something new. Sure, there are always aesthetic rebellions, (take the recent rise in hand-drawn, messy graphics as a rejection of slick computer graphics). But these tend to form easy to copy visual trends. In long-lasting revolutionary terms they hold little potency. The reality is that so many designers spend so much of their time following a brief, tweaking a corporate logo, designing 'on-brand', me included. To make matters worse, you're not always designing for a client you believe in. 'I've done them all,' joked a colleague of mine, 'Mining companies, weapons manufacturers, oil producers. I've had to leave my ethics at home when I'm designing,' he said wryly. A revolt seems inevitable from people with such freethinking potential.

This is the spark that has set off the fire for the new design rebels. And the same way that the new social rebels are seen as do-gooders, the new design rebels want to make a positive change in society. Cristiano Toraldo di Francia, one of the founders of Superstudio pronounced, 'It is the designer who must attempt to re-evaluate his role in the nightmare he helped to conceive.'

Today that re-evaluation has come in the form of an anti-globalisation, socially conscious design movement, that takes 'No-Logo' as it's bible and Kalle Lasn, editor of Adbusters, as it's pope. As protagonists of the movement, Adbusters Culture Jammers Network describe their aim as 'To topple existing power structures and forge a major shift in the way we will live in the 21st century.' Translating their passions to the professional world, Kalle Lasn and Tibor Kalman re-issued Ken Garland's 1964 *First Things First Manifesto* in 2000. Signed by 33 design heavyweights, and printed in magazines across the design world, it proposes 'A reversal of priorities in favour of more useful, lasting and democratic forms of communication.' 'Consumerism is running uncontested,' they say, 'it must be challenged by other perspectives expressed, in part, through the visual languages and resources of design.' Taking this to heart, the University of Richmond, Virginia, established a course literally entitled 'Design Rebels' teaching design for social responsibility. 'Designers have a powerful skill,' says Noah Scalin, the creator and instructor of the class. 'Questioning what you're doing as a job is really rebellious.'

Wow! Toppling power structures, rebel-rousing manifestos, raising big questions for society. Makes you want to put down your mouse, run out and join up straight away! But there's a pattern forming amongst these new school forms of rebellion that our old school rebels suffered. Sure, they don't follow the pattern encouraged by the majority of their peers. However, abstinence movements have received over $120 million in funding since 2003 from the US government, and under Bush are being promoted as the only form of sex education in one third of US states. There has also been worry that some young Muslims increased religious zeal is due to having fallen prey to fundamentalist Imams or trying to avoid persecution in their rough suburban estates. Even Straight Edgers have experienced this 'follow the leader' style conformism. McKay became so agitated that he re released a version of 'Out of Step' with the words, 'this is no set of rules, I'm not telling you what to say or do.' The culture jamming movement is in danger of meeting that inevitable situation. For instance, the Design Rebels course is so called because it 'sounded appealing to students'. Even the notion of a manifesto for all to follow sits uneasily with the spirit of individuality and freethinking promoted by the movement.

These forms of convention show a hole in rebellion in general. How many of our rebels, be it the new conformists or old school activists, are true radicals

01
Borja Martinez
Pige-on (Football Pitch)
Chalk on sidewalk
Barcelona 2004

and how many feel compelled to join the crowd? Two million people turned out to join the anti-war marches in England last year. But I remember it being a case of many people tagging along just because their friends were. It almost became a fun day out for all the family, rather than a passionate act of protest. It's indicative of how acts of rebellion inevitably turn into acts of convention. Because real rebels are different and because they don't care what anyone else thinks, we think they're cool. And once something's seen as cool, everyone wants a piece of the action. You could call it anarchy for cache's sake.

There's a fundamental problem with this pattern of the rebel subculture becoming mainstream. So maybe a true rebellion is not an en-masse movement, but a personal fight. Maybe that's what my father meant. Real rebels don't fear going it alone; they don't need other people to act as a comfort blanket. There's an element of personal risk involved in a revolt that's lost once more people join the

cause. I never wanted to smoke because it never appealed. I never wanted to drink much because I didn't like the taste. Above all, I didn't want to follow what other people cajoled me into doing just to fit in. So maybe in my own acceptable way, I'm a bit more rebellious than I first thought.

* * *

Rosanna Vitiello is a graphic designer and an occassional writer, she rebels, in her own way, and works in London. Borja Martinez is a graphic designer, he disturbs pigeons and works in Barcelona.

163

Why should we bother talking about a mail order catalogue that was first published more than thirty years ago?.

THE PAPERBACK TOOLBOX

Text by Aficionado + Constance F Iker

The first Whole Earth Catalog was published in 1968. It was the brainchild of Stewart Brand, an American biologist and urban hipster who thought of it as his contribution to the efforts of his friends that were 'starting a new civilisation, out there in the sticks', a catalogue of *tools* that 'owed nothing to the suppliers, and everything to its users'. It started in garages and borrowed offices, and it went on to sell several million copies. It made the works and the ideas of a range of radical intellectuals, scientists, educators, and political thinkers - from R Buckminster Fuller to the Black Panthers and Ken Kesey - accessible to a large number of people. It also set the precedent for Brand's later ventures (from the first 'Hackers' Conference' in '84 to the more recent 'Long Now Foundation' and the 'All Species Inventory'). The title refers to a campaign that Brand had run a couple of years earlier, badges with the slogan 'Why haven't we seen a picture of the whole earth yet?', which are rumoured to have gotten through to NASA and prompted the release of the first pictures of the whole earth taken from space, which in turn, as legend would have it, helped raise ecological awareness and kick-started the 'green' movement.

A Review-in-Progress

Aficionado: What made 6 million hippies, ready to start a new world, subscribe to a mail-order catalogue? …maybe it had to do with what the catalogue had to offer, with the products…

Constance F Iker: The catalogue in question didn't offer any 'products' that were any way exceptional, in my opinion, but what it offered was a way of engaging with existence…you only had to look at the cover of each copy and you knew you were travelling in a different terrain…

A: The famous pictures of the whole earth…I suppose it even begins with the title itself, the WHOLE EARTH CATALOG, it suggests that you're about to enter a world of sorts…maybe the individual 'products' ('tools') were not exceptional in themselves, but it is in the way they come together in the catalogue, in the fact that they're together that creates something a bit more interesting, both as a cultural proposition and as a resource.

C F Iker: Yes, 'access to tools' the subtitle and maybe the key to unlocking the intentions of the people involved, but before we delve inside its pages, I think it

01

The famous Apollo 8 picture of Earthrise over the Moon that established our planetary facthood and beauty and rareness (dry moon, barren space) and began to bend human conciousness.

The Last Whole Earth Catalog 1971

01-02

The first known picture of the whole earth from space was probably taken during the Apollo 4 mission in 1967 and released later that same year. In those, urban legend would have it, days it took a campaign to get these pictures out to the public, these days a picture database at the NASA website makes them available for public download and -use in a variety of resolutions.

Source: NASA

It begins to say that even if we're trying to create a new world, or a new/different way of being in the world; we should learn first to make use of what this world has made available to us

worth just pausing a second to reflect on its subversive qualities… in so much as subverting the idea of a 'shopping catalogue'. Shopping catalogues don't usually have such well informed commentary neither do they give direct contact to suppliers. Was the Whole Earth Catalog a middle-ground; a broker between 'the hippies' and the 'the man'? Something necessary in trying to keep society together, whilst moving in our many different directions?

A: … 'burning the bridges, not the libraries' … I think the way the Whole Earth Catalog takes on the idea of the mail-order catalogue and the notion of shopping shows an interesting path to talk about cultural and social change. It begins to say that even if we're trying to create a new world, or a new/different way of being in the world; we should learn first to make use of what this world has made available to us. It proposes a subtler, long-term change as opposed to the direct confrontation of previous eras, evolution instead of revolution. A good example of this it's also the way in which 'products' become 'tools' in the catalogue, you've mentioned this before, but also the way in which the conventional idea of 'tool' is redefined, we could even quote:

> The Whole Earth Catalog functions as an evaluation and access device. With it; the user should know better what is worth getting and where and how to do the getting. An item is listed in the Whole Earth Catalog if it is deemed:
> 1—useful as a tool
> 2—relevant to independent education
> 3—high quality or low cost
> 4—easily available by mail
> Whole Earth Catalog listings are continually revised according to the experience and suggestions of Whole Earth Catalog users and staff."

C F Iker: Past the cover, now we come to the over-arching concern of the editors with the structure. Each edition of the Whole Earth Catalog began, self-consciously, with looking at the latest explorations in ecosystem awareness, holistic views within biology and nature etc. This was very important to the whole enterprise. It was also widely read by both young and old alike…Whole Systems/Biodiversity. Land Use. Shelter.

Industry. Craft. Community. Nomadics. Communications. Learning…and lest we be so foolish…the 'Last Whole Earth Catalog' of 1971 (it was meant to be the last but an 'Epilog' was published in '74 and the catalogue reappeared sparingly and irregularly throughout the 70s and until year 2000, which is the latest known edition) finished with a 'How to do your own Whole Earth Catalog'. But as is immediately apparent from the section order… prevalence was given to the 'holistic' first… 'let's look at the big picture first, and then continue on from there' …and from there was basic economics - Food. Shelter. Clothing. But with the emphasis firmly on self-sufficiency.

A: There's maybe a more abstract set of things going on with the structure, not even in the sequence itself but in the 'style' of structuring, again the emphasis is always in a certain kind of honesty. The catalogue continuously explains itself, from the choice of imagery on the cover, to the mission statements at the beginning, all editorial decisions are always explained and shared, this also shows how it became a different kind of format, the Whole Earth Catalog 'editorialised' the form of the catalogue. That was, to my knowledge, truly new, and that strategy alone makes it relevant to today's media, which is increasingly populated by data-driven formats like catalogues, archives, compilations, etc. It maybe suggests strategies to enrich those formats beyond mere 'choice'. It is worth remembering that this 'editorial' approach came from somewhere, it followed from this holistic perspective. They simply put their money where their mouth was, and applied the advice they were supplying to the making of the catalogue itself. It was a tool about tools - the catalogue satisfied the same requirements a 'tool' needed to in order to be included in the catalogue. It was a system about systems, and a self-sufficient enterprise about self-sufficiency. They published their accounts at the end of every catalogue, explained what happened to the cover price, and how the catalogue was run…that in itself became an example of successful self-sufficiency at work. Every aspect of the catalogue was accountable and every decision answerable to the same criteria as any of the things within it …

Thirty years have passed, and the Whole Earth Catalog has not only remained relevant as a resource, but it has also acquired new value…it has become a toolbox of strategies for independent publishing and distribution, it has also become a significant historical document, a witness to the efforts of a generation to do things in their own way, to propose an alternative, to make a difference.

* * *

After 1974 the Whole Earth Catalog became the Co-Evolution Quarterly,
a journal filled with lengthy articles on the same subjects covered by the catalogue,
… it changed its name in 1985 to the Whole Earth Review,
and again in 1996 to the Whole Earth Magazine
under which it is published to this day. (www.wholeearthmag.com)
Kevin Kelly became the editor of the CoEvolution Quarterly in 1984
and took on the task of publishing new catalogs after Stewart Brand left,
he later went on to become the first editor of Wired,
in 2003 he began publishing his 'tool' reviews online. (www.kk.org/cooltools/)

We were about to begin the first of our three walks. Our journeys around the streets of London are intended as an act of contrition, and we feel as repentant pilgrims must have felt.

WALKING IN CIRCLES
—
IN SEARCH OF A CULTURAL REVOLUTION

Text + Photography
by Maziar Raein + Nick Robertson

The origins of our sin had taken form a week before when during a drunken session, we had started ranting. About what is not exactly clear now, but I suppose you could call it popular culture. Our experience, like that of many of our contemporaries, is a sense of alienation from what is being dished up to us by the media; from the dreary pap of television programmes like Big Brother, to the endless and mind numbing manufactured effluence, pretending to be music which pours out of cynical hit factories.

Walking has natural a pace and is conducive to thinking, so we would walk to order our ideas, attempting to sound out the future by looking at the past. We planned the walks around London, deciding that the structure of each walk had to start at a site of former culturally revolutionary significance and lead to its contemporary nemesis as well as being long enough to allow us to reach a conclusion. After all we had to give ourselves distance to think. For us the term revolutionary is synonymous with rebelliousness, and there is little evidence of it at present in our popular culture.

The modern definition of the term 'Popular Culture' has become synonymous with entertainment, but for centuries, even before it was coined in the 1960s [01], it referred to the popular and democratic concept of public education, through access to knowledge, ushered in by the founding of public libraries. Our first walk started at the former site of the greatest public Library of all, the British Library.

Walk 1: From Dome to Dome

We are standing in the British Museum and are looking the remains of what was once the most significant repository of books in the world; The British Library Reading Room [02]. As we stand in the centre of the space and look up at the large domed ceiling, it is hard not to get the feeling that you are inside an engine. Some big blue and gold thought bubble containing nearly 150 years of brilliant and revolutionary ideas. The novelist Virginia Woolf suggested the British library reading room was 'an enormous mind…hoarding beyond the power of any single mind to posses it.' (Jacob's Room 1922)

If there is anywhere in England, which can be said to be a revolutionary space then this, is it. Completed in 1847 and the brainchild of Antonio Panizzi this was a genuinely unique and radical undertaking. His vision was to create a repository of publicly accessible knowledge containing every publication in the English language, a feat it still continues to achieve 150 years later. Very soon after its opening the entire area around the museum began to become a centre of esoteric learning and occult practices. This was not only unique but also slightly dangerous to the established order. This influx of radical thinkers chose the Reading Room as their incubator and they came from all areas from literature to Science and religion. It was here that Darwin worked on his 'Origin of the Species', which caused total scientific and religious upheaval.

Almost every figure to have made a serious impression in the last two centuries has used this room, from the mainstream academics to the increasingly radical thinkers of the day. Hall Caine describes, '…a shabby coat here, a shiny hat there…Dreaming dreams they are never to see realized, living on hoping, buoying themselves up with visions.' (The Eternal City, 1901) Karl Marx used the library every day for 30 years working on many projects including 'Das Kapital'. International communism was practically conceived in this room with as stream of regulars including Vladimir Ilyich Lenin who applied for his reader's ticket under the alias of Jacob Richter. It was Lenin who arranged for Leon Trotsky to become a member, again under an alias now unknown.

It is perhaps significant that the Museum Trustees of the time withdrew the second edition of Cundall's 'Dictionary of explosives' from the shelves, striking the tome from the catalogue!

As a national institution the British Library is a massive repository of information, it does not attempt to evaluate knowledge, and in a sense (a Borgesian sense) it is a representation of our collective memory.

We leave the building and set off east down Great Russell Street. We have a long walk to another now out of use dome, which for all of the 360 days of 2000 also claimed the distinction of being a repository of knowledge, British ingenuity and national pride.

SHOULD <u>ALL</u> LIBRARIES BE BURNED?

We are heading for Bugsby Marshes or 'The East Greenwich Peninsula' as it was re-branded in the late 1990s. This area has for much of the last 100 years, been seen as an example of the mistakes of 19th century industrialists. Stretches of dead swampy land contaminated by Molasses, guano and all the other toxicants bled into the mud through the years of industry took on a new lease of life at the end of the last century when the site was cleaned and developed to accommodate 'The Millennium Dome'.

The immense white belly with its yellow legs sticking up into the air is visible well before we get anywhere near it. It is certainly big. It was conceived on big ideas as well. Originally intended to be along the same lines as the Great Exhibitions of 1851 and the Festival of Britain in 1951, it was to be a celebration of all the achievements, which made Britain great in the areas of commerce, science, architecture, art and industry. That was the idea anyway.

We eventually arrive having made our way through the empty landscape ear marked for commercial development and stand at the base of the tent. The thing is closed and shut up tight. The dome seems oddly at home in this barren environment, there is no sign of the promised revitalisation. Its presence is an imposition on the area, a desolate legacy to the Greenwich Peninsula, in contrast with the rich legacy of the Reading Room and the explosion of bookshops and publishing houses which still linger in the area.

We can only rely on memories of the Dome experience but they are quite enough. What started as an exhibition of British achievement was swiftly rail-roaded by big international conglomerates and what we ended up with was a confusion of trade show and fun fair. A lack of time and an excess of spending produced a half realized corporate make over which drained huge amounts of public money to provide a showcase for multinationals.

Entering the Dome was like entering an aircraft hanger, a looming, unattractive projection screen. This was a space, which exploited knowledge without contributing to its furtherment. It was above all an intellectually safe and controlled environment, which deliberately pandered to a culture that valued brands and consuming over ideas and intellectual effort.

What was left was an exhibition, which was put into the hands of designers and meddlesome politicians, producing a confused and myopic vision of the present. It cast knowledge in the role of 'infotainment' and in so doing, completely lost the opportunity to communicate to the public. This is the antithesis of the Reading Room and a flaccid, modern attempt to emulate it.

It is perhaps significant that the Museum Trustees of the time withdrew the second edition of Grendall's *Dictionary of Explosives* from the shelves, striking the tome from the catalogue!

---

[01]
As a term, 'Popular culture' was first used to distinguish between High Culture, (with a Capital C); as represented through high literature, fine art, classical music, opera etc. rather than the emergent youth culture of post-war America. This emerging group - the American teenager - with its affluent and disposable income concern themselves with rock & roll, fashion and films created a social phenomena, which was played out daily on the radio and television. Its transference to the swinging London of the 1960s saw an explosion of creativity, the effects of which are still recognised.

[02]
In the heart of London two types of institution exemplify this historical, phenomenon, the museum and the department store. Neil Cummings and Marysia Lewandowska, demonstrated this relationship in their book *The Value of Things*, both these institutions were importers and displayers of goods from elsewhere (often the British Colonies) and both ascribed value to the objects they stored and handled - this is vase from Greece and it is of value, we shall make it the object of scholarly investigation and display to the public as high culture or this is a vase from India and we shall value it and display it to the public, making it an object of popular culture.

Walk 2: Jerusalem to Bankside

The phrase 'marriage of heaven and hell' refers to the coming together of two unlikely forces, a demonic marriage and our second walk through London revolves around this idea. A third dome is on our minds as we get off the tube at Kennington, that of the Royal Albert Hall on the last nigh of the Proms when the nationalistic ritual of singing 'Jerusulum' calls the words of William Blake up from the past. We are outside No 13 Hercules road, Lambeth, the site of the home of this artist, poet and mystic.

If the reading room provides us with a revolutionary location, then Blake gives us a truly visionary artist. It is ironic that one of the most revolutionary and influential artists of his generation was misunderstood and considered a madman by his contemporaries. Even today when the Albert Hall promenaders brandish their Union Jacks and sing Jerusalem in stirring tones we see all too clearly that is his work is still misunderstood.

'It is hardly likely that he (Blake) would have approved of his words being used as a celebration of national consciousness. He was an anti monarchist, he did not support the established church, he was a dissenter in every sense.' - Peter Ackroyd

William Blake moved in to this address in 1790 and set up residence as well as his studio, in October that year he published a prospectus addressed to the public, with the aim of selling his illuminated books and prints. His 'Method of Printing which combines the Painter and the Poet' was an attempt to distribute directly to the public and not just to an elite. It was part of the egalitarian ethos that is a strong thread in British artistic and literary traditions. Its most significant manifestation of recent years was the fanzine during the height of the punk era.

The previous year, 1789 was a significant date in European history, since it was during this year that the French Revolution started and Blake like many artists of his time, responded to its call. Blake believed that the spiritual and socio-political world were linked and saw a parallel between his personal vision of a spiritual development that deploys the human beings creative energy, and the forces of the French revolution which were directing social change. Blake held this belief with such passion and conviction that many commentators still see Blake's work as being relevant to contemporary culture. However, the idyllic scene of the Vale of Lambeth turned into a darker and more sinister period for Blake and his wife Catherine, when their revolutionary views led to the possible accusation of political sedition and

Today the impression of change is enough and we believe the illusion. The radicalism of the YBAs is nothing more than the garish mask of the po- seur. The works displayed at the Saatchi Gallery are an incarnation of the New Academy, which has assimilated the dynamism of a whole generation

imprisonment.

Blake also opposed the artistic establishment of the day and a constant state of war existed between him and the Royal Academy (whose figure-head was the aging Joshua Reynolds), which was originally located in Somerset House, across the river from his Lambeth residence. The Academy's role was to prescribe, produce and endorse the 'Art' and 'Artists' of the period to oversee art that served the establishment and confirmed the role of its existing elite. This institution still exists today, it delivers to us with an endless series of blockbuster shows, amply visited by the blue rinse brigade of the home counties and contains an art school which is well attended by the sons and daughters of the great and good. Ironically, this very Academy was the host of the Sensation show, which launched The Young British Artists (YBA) internationally.

A short walk of a few hundred meters from Hercules Road to the south end of Westminster Bridge and we find ourselves at the new spiritual home of British art, the Saatchi gallery, installed in the former home of London County Council. The Young British Artists (YBA) as it has been branded, since the mid 90s, represented the cutting edge of British art supporting the enfant terribles of the scene and giving art a much larger cultural presence and popular appeal.

They have long been seen as the revolutionary bad boys (and girls) of art, superficially at least, Blakian in appearance. However, it is perhaps no accident that the leading organizer of YBA art, one may even say the curator of the movement is an adverting guru. Charles Saatchi is someone who is well versed in the packaging and selling of an idea, and in many ways it is appropriate that he is the current patron of British establishment-art. In every age the main patrons of the establishment artists, have reflected their needs in the art they support. This can be seen in the art of the Royal Academy in Blake's time and the religious art of earlier times when the church was the great patron.

The work from this stable of artists is aesthetically simple, clean and employs the language of graphics and the media. It is clever but in an advertising, one-liner kind of way which while being occasionally thought provoking, is accessible to most of its viewers. Not withstanding this, as a body of artists their work is held up in art schools, displayed in state sponsored galleries like the Tate Modern (only 10 minutes further down the Thames) and discussed ad nausea in scholarly art publications. Despite the claim that YBA work is revolutionary, would it be possible to conceive any one of them being considered dangerous by the State today? The abhorrence of the war in Iraq, the injustice AIDS in Africa, the slaughter of democracy in the Far East, have the YBA's ever made a nodding acknowledgement of this? Is this the work of a revolutionary movement or a revisionist makeover?

As we walk through the beautiful wood panelled building filled with colourful canvases, tanks full of formaldehyde, and enormous sculptural pieces, it is difficult to see beyond the walls at what else could be happening. This is very much the art establishment. This is what Blake raged against. This is the accepted face of British art.

Despite using a language of advertising, the media and the people, the YBAs are an exclusive group who are totally at odds with the Blakian egalitarian ethos. Rather than producing work, which was directly accessible to the people as Blake did, the only access we have to it is through a gallery, the arbiter of taste. It is the art of the privileged affirmed and endorsed by the elite and powerful.

The social mechanism employed by the cultural elite which makes this possible, is that of assimilation. Assimilation is the process through which another can incorporate the ideas, thoughts, activities and traits of one group. Through this sophisticated integration of the new by the old, the establishment demonstrates that it has learnt the lessons of the sixties, when the radicalism of the young began to challenge the order of things. Today the impression of change is enough and we believe the illusion. The radicalism of the YBAs is nothing more than the garish mask of the poseur. The works displayed in the Saatchi Gallery are an incarnation of the New Academy, which has assimilated the dynamism of a whole generation.

Walk 3 Marquee to HMV

Heading down the Charing Cross Road on our third and final walk we see a taxi glide by, it is covered in Damien Hirst's dots and it's advertising the Tate Modern gallery on Bankside. We are walking down Charing Cross Road to the beginning of our third walk.

Standing on the corner of Charing Cross Road and Old Compton Street there are two sites within a 100-meter radius, which are signifiers of moments in popular culture. Across the Charing Cross Road from the old Saint Martins art school (now Central Saint Martins) building is a block of flats in which Derek Jarman lived in for most of the Eighties before his move to Dungeness. Of the generation that just preceded Punk, Jarman tapped into much of the energy of that era and was probably the most

influential British filmmaker of the period. His method of filmmaking was simple but effective, a mixture of DIY and poetry, using readily available Super-8 cameras, he would shoot footage (sometimes arbitrarily) based around a theme and recompile the material into a poetic or narrative form in the editing stages. His approach was reminiscent of a home made poster knocking around in 1976, it was a horizontal A4 sheet with cut outs of three guitar chords illustrations and scrawled underneath were the words; 'Now you've learnt them start your own band'.

The DIY spirit also manifested itself in the Marquee club in Greek Street, where Punk bands regularly played in 1976. Punk was a revolution in music and fashion, which was the last moment of clarity for British youth movements. Britain was in economic and social crisis with mass unemployment, trade disputes, and a feeling of tired defeat and deep resentment. Punk fed off this negative energy and in turn, reflected it. Their philosophy of energy over technique, get up and do it yourself was a reaction to the state of England but also to the over technique based music and fashion to the manufactured stadium rock of bands like YES, Wishboneash and Pink Floyd. Their clothes were held together with safety pins and they just picked up the guitars and thrashed them.

The magical quality of music resides in the fact that it acts as a transitional medium between the internal world (especially of a sixteen year old) and the external world. It becomes a voice through which one can express the incoherent and half recognised emotions one is feeling. Punk was able to do this; it expressed the internal frustrations of that generation.

The important point was that this was a self-initiated youth sub-culture. It was decentralizing control from record companies, fashion houses, in short every part of the youth consumer producers. This made it dangerous. The anger expressed in punk, the call for Anarchy, the swearing on television, the heroin, the murder, the suicide, 'God save the queen, it's a fascist regime', the lack of fear, the explosion of feeling, the fury finding expression, the tribal unity, all conspired to frighten the established social order. The press denounced punk, the Government took measures to suppress it, moralist preached and administrators legislated, but punk swept the country. It was a purely reactionary movement in which frustration and dissatisfaction found a cultural expression.

We continue walking up Charring Cross road and as we turn left onto Oxford Street, we reflect that punk is by no means an isolated phenomenon. It has been repeated throughout history. Even the romantics can,

Nostalgia, 'the British disease' is the establishment's 'opiate of the people'. It looks at our cultural heritage and comfortingly pats us on the back, reminding us how innovative we have been in the past and glossing over the fact that we are now living in an age that lacks confidence in itself and in the future

CAN ANY STATEMENT BE MADE THAT ISN'T A <u>FASHION</u> STATEMENT?

to a certain extent, be seen as the punk peacocks of their day. They were artists, they rebelled against artistic conventions, they dressed outrageously (Shelley), they were promiscuous (Byron), they were drug abusers, (Coleridge & De Quincey). Above all the establishment feared them. Byron was forced into self-imposed exile. They were 'mad, bad and dangerous to know'. The very street we are walking down: Oxford Street was the home of the youthful Thomas De Quincey and the setting for much of his 'Confessions of an English Opium Eater'. This was a connection not missed by Malcolm MacLaren, the creator of The Sex Pistols and arguably the father of Punk when he wrote a history of Oxford Street in the 1990s.

Oxford Street has become a reflection of what is worst in British culture today. The street furniture and signage screams out its lack of confidence in the present. Shop after shop proclaims itself as either an American corporate import (Footlocker and Borders etc.) or a sad heritage industry outlet. In the heritage culture of 2004 you can buy pictures of Mohican wearing punks and send them home to your mom - YEH it's really wild here!

After being pushed and shoved down the street, we come to the conclusion of our walk: the HMV store, Oxford Street. If one were going to find evidence of the existence of a youth sub-culture in operation today, it would be in the music of today. What are people listening to? We head for the Indie section with the not unreasonable idea that, as in the eighties when the term was coined, we will find something a bit underground, at least by HMV's standards. What we found were The Kings of Leon, The Flaming Lips, The Strokes, The Datsuns, The Dandy Warhols, The White Stripes, row upon row of rehashed post-modern regurgitation. We took some over to the listening-stand and the situation proved worse than we

had imagined. Take The Eagles and add a dash of AC/DC, mix a pinch of Neil Young for seasoning and a splash of Velvet Underground and hey presto…we have a mash of things we have already heard 20 years ago and are comfortable with. No voice, no individuality, no new ideas at all.

We look further a field and find Gareth Gates, Busted, Girls Aloud, Will Young…it's time to leave, we run for it…It's nearly time for Pop Idol!

After our last walk it is easy to reflect that in the world of the ready made, be it British art, music or popular youth culture is no longer a force in society. It is a product ready for consumption and allowing little room for the individual's identity to shine through. All interaction has become a manufactured experience, within a programmed set of responses rather than a lived experience. We are sold culture retrospectively. Like Punk, our culture is now part of the Great British heritage trail. It is part of the romantic texture of eccentric and colourful England and we can buy into that nostalgia without offending any one.

Nostalgia, 'the British disease' is the establishment's 'opiate of the people'. It looks at our cultural heritage and comfortingly pats us on the back, reminding us how innovative we have been in the past and glossing over the fact that we are now living in an age that lacks confidence in itself and the future. As the latest Nineties fashion revival looms round the corner we can almost see the back of our heads as we revolve round the cultural cycle and now, we can no longer discern revolving from revolution.

* * *

Maziar Raein is the Head of Context
on the BA Graphic Design course
at Central St Martins College of Art + Design
(he does NOT live in Hampstead
and has no children)
Nick Robertson is the founder of Wordsalad,
a design studio based in London,
and he also lectures at
Central St Martins College of Art + Design

171

MUNCH CRUNCH

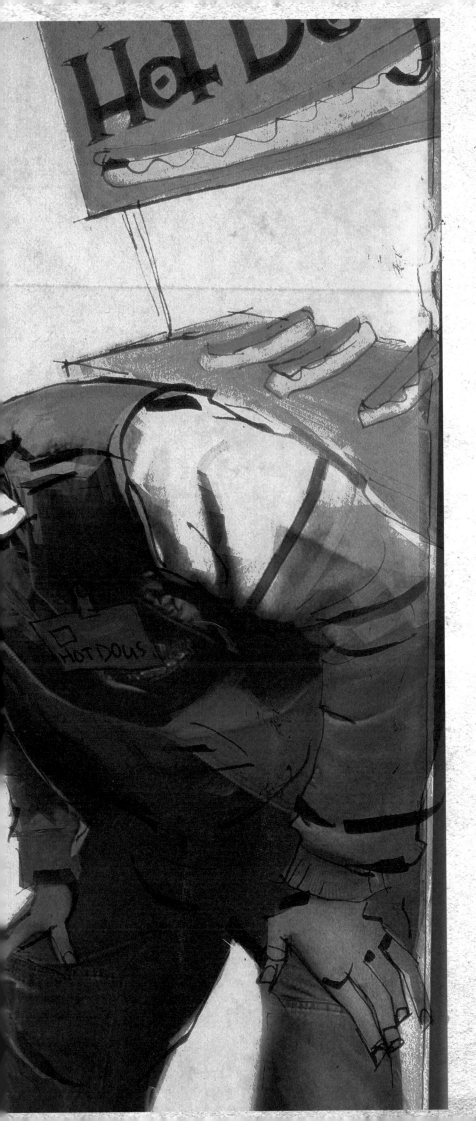

H OWIE HOWIE
LOST A FEW FINGERS
WORKING FOR HIS BUTCHER DAD,

AND EVEN IF HE KNEW
IT WASN'T ALL MOOSE MEAT,

IT WAS THE BEST FOOD HE'D EVER HAD.

DARK TALES
ONLY TO READ AT HOME

GRAPHIC is distributed by:

Australia
Tower Books
Unit 2, 17 Rodborough Road
Frenchs Forest, NSW 2086
T +62 2 9975 5566
F +62 2 9975 5599
E towerbks@zipworld.com.au
www.foliograph.com.au

Belgium
Bookstores
Exhibitions International
Kol. Begaultlaan 17
B-3012 Leuven
T +32 16 296 900
F +32 16 284 540
E orders@exhibitionsinternational.be
www.exhibitionsinternational.be

Other
Imapress
Brugstraat 51
B-2300 Turnhout

France
Critique Livres Distribution SAS
BP 93-24 rue Malmaison
93172 Bagnolet Cedex
T +33 1 4360 3910
F +33 1 4897 3706
E critiques.livres@wanadoo.fr

Germany
Bookstores
Sales representative South Germany:
Stefan Schempp
Augsburger Strasse 12
D-80337 München
T +49 89-230 77 737
F +49 89-230 77 738
E verlagsvertretung.schempp@t-online.de

North Germany
Sales Representative
Kurt Salchli
Marienburger Strasse 10
D-10405 Berlin
T +49 30 4171 7530
F +49 30 4171 7531
E salchli@t-online.de

Germany, Austria & Switzerland
Distribution/Auslieferung
GVA Gemeinsame Verlagsauslieferung Göttingen
Anna-Vandenhoeck-Ring 36
37081 Göttingen
Germany
T +49 551 487 177
F +49 051 413 92
E krause@gva-verlage.de

Other
IPS Pressevertrieb GmbH
Carl-Zeiss-Strasse 5
D-53340 Meckenheim
T +49 22 258801 122
F +49 22 258801 199
E publishing@ips-pressevertrieb.de
www.ips-pressevertrieb.de

Indonesia
Aksara
Jalan Kemang Raya 8b
Jakarta 12730
T +62 21 7199 288
F +62 21 7199 282
E info@aksara.com
www.aksara.com

Italy
Idea srl
Via Lago Trasimeno, 23/2 (ZI)
36015 Schio (VI)
T +39 455 576 574
F +39 445 577 764
E info@ideabooks.it
www.ideabooks.it

Red Edizioni Sas
Viale Prampolini 110
41100 Modena
T +39 59 212 792
F +39 59 4392 133
E info@redonline.it

Librimport Sas
Via Biondelli 9
20141 Milano
T +39 2 8950 1422
F +39 2 8950 2811
E librimport@libero.it

Japan
Shimada Yosho
T.Place, 5-5-25, Minami-Aoyama, Minato-Ku
Tokyo, 107-0062
T +81 3 3407 3937
F +81 3 3407 0989
E sales@shimada.attnet.ne.jp

Korea
Beatboy Inc.
Kangnam-Ku Shinsa-Dong 666-11
Baegang Building 135-897
Seoul
T +82 2 3444 8367
F +82 2 541 8358
E yourbeatboy@hanmail.net

Malaysia
How & Why Sdn Bhd
101A, Jalan SS2/24
47300 Petaling Jaya
Selangor
T +60 3 7877 4800
F +60 3 7877 4600
E info@howwwhy.com
www.howwwhy.com

Mexico
LHR Distribuidor de Libros
Calle 11 No. 69-1
Col.V. Gomez Farias Mexico
D.F. 15010 Mexico
T +52 55 5785 8996
F +52 55 5785 7816
E lhrlibro@prodigy.net.mx
www.lhrlibros.com

The Netherlands
Bookstores
Betapress BV
Burg. Krollaan 14
5126 PT Gilze
T +31 161 457 800
F +31 161 457 224

Other
BIS Publishers
Herengracht 370-372
1016 CH Amsterdam
T +31 20 524 7560
F +31 20 524 7557
E bis@bispublishers.nl
www.bispublishers.nl

Russia
Design Books
3 Maly Kislovsky Lane office 315
Moscow 103009
T +7 095 203 65 94
F +7 095 203 65 94

Scandinavia
(Denmark, Finland, Norway, Sweden)
Sales Representative
Bo Rudin
Box 5058
SE-165 11 Hasselby
Sweden
T +46 8 894 080
F +46 8 388 320
E rudins@swipnet.se

Singapore
Basheer Graphic Books
Block 231, Bain Street
#04–19 Bras Basah Complex
180231 Singapore
T +65 336 0810
F +65 334 1950

Page One Pte Ltd
20 Kaki Bukit View
Kaki Bukit Techpark II
415956 Singapore
T +65 744 2088
F +65 744 2088
E pageone@singnet.com.sg

Spain
ACTAR
Roca i Batlle 2 i 4
08023 Barcelona
T +34 93 418 77 59
F +34 93 418 67 07
E info@actar-mail.com
www.actar.es

Taiwan
Long Sea International Book Co.,Ltd.
1/F No. 204 Si Wei Rd
Taipei 106 Taiwan ROC
T +886 2 2706 6838
F +886 2 2706 6109
E thfang@ms16.hinet.net
www.longsea.co.tw

Turkey
Evrensel Grafikir Yayincilik
Gulbahar Mahl
Gayret SK No:11
80300-01 Mecidiyekoy/Istanbul
T +90 212 356 7276
F +90 212 356 7278
E evrensely@superonline.com

United Kingdom
Bookstores
Airlift Book Company
8 The Arena
Mollison Avenue
Enfield, Middlesex EN3 7NL
T +44 20 8804 0400
F +44 20 8804 0044
E info@airlift.co.uk
www.airlift.co.uk

Other
Comag Specialist
Tavistock Works
Tavistock Road
West Drayton
Middlesex UB7 7QX
T +44 1895 433 800
F +44 1895 433 801
E andy.hounslow@comag.co.uk

USA/Canada
Lords News International
133 Jefferson Avenue
Jersey City, NJ 07306
T +1 201 798 2555
F +1 201 798 5335
lordnewsinc@hotmail.com
www.lordsusa.com

USA/West Coast
Trucatriche
3800 Main Street Suite 8
Chula Vista, CA 91911
California
T +1 619 426 2690
F +1 619 426 2695
E info@trucatriche.com

Subscriptions to graphic
(all prices include airmail)

1 year (4 issues)
◯ Europe EUR80/GBP55
◯ USA/Canada USD105
◯ Other countries USD125

2 years (8 issues)
◯ Europe EUR149/GBP103
◯ USA/Canada USD195
◯ Other countries USD225

Students
(valid only with a copy of your student
registration form)

1 year (4 issues)
◯ Europe EUR63/GBP43.50
◯ USA/Canada USD90
◯ Other countries USD100

Fax this form to:
+31 20 524 75 57

or send to:
graphic
Herengracht 370–372
1016 CH Amsterdam
The Netherlands

code GR/BZ/06

Payment (for prompt delivery please pay by credit card)
◯ Please charge my: ◯ Visa ◯ AmEx ◯ Euro/Master
◯ Please invoice me/my company
   (first issue will be sent on receipt of payment)

Mr/Ms   Name _____   Surname _____

Card number _____   CVC−2 Code * _____

Expiry date _____   Signature _____

Company _____

Address ** _____

City _____   Postcode/Zip _____

Country _____   Telephone _____

Email _____   Fax _____

*: Please add your CVC−2 code (the last 3 digits of the number printed
on the signature strip on the back of your card) if paying by Mastercard.

**: Please also attach details of card billing address if different from delivery address.

SCHNEIDER
PAPIER

Cover printed on
250 g/m² Luxocard I

papergrades used in this issue are
ed out of the international collection
neider Papier...

ore information:
schneider-papier.nl
l 0031 30 6629222

PEOPLE AND PAPER

Obituaries

The forefather of sound political thinking

Juan Pablo Fernandez

Juan Pablo Fernandez, who died earlier this month at the age of 86, was without doubt one of Yorkshire's finest Latin dictators. His passion and commitment in driving through his policies – of social and economic reform through the power of latin music – during the height of his political career was a turning point in modern political thought. 'He was a true visionary,' said Neil Kinnock of his closest friend. 'He replaced flat caps and whippets with sombreros and maracas, and we loved it. He will be sadly missed.' Not least by his local constituency in Bubwith, who even to this day can be seen wearing their ponchos with pride.

Born in Paraguay in 1926, the only child to Vincente and Cristina Fernandez – bean farmers from a small village close to the Brazilian border – the young Juan Pablo spent his formative years working as child labour in his father's bean factory. The hardship and struggle during this time was lightened only by the touring Afro-Cuban group, 'Roberto Roena Y Su's Apollo Sound', who held a regular friday afternoon spot at the bean factory. Employed by Vincente, their job was to boost moral among the workers as they counted beans.

In 1940, eager to explore a world beyond beans, Juan Pablo took the unprecedented step of seeking legal advice, divorcing himself from his parents and putting himself up for adoption. Dorothy and Cyril Burgess from Wakefield were to become his new parents in 1942, after visiting the small village of Juan Pablo's birth and seeing his 'adoption wanted' poster on a tree. Dorothy and Cyril took their new son back with them to England and it was here that Fernandez was to find his social and political conscience. In his 1986 unofficial biography of Fernandez, 'The Grim North is Alight With a Latin Passion', the social and political historian Marcus Selby wrote: 'for a child like Juan Pablo to be taken from his bean counting duties and be placed into the exciting new environment of Wakefield could only have had a prominent social and psychological effect on the young Fernandez; it was an environment in which he now had to re-adapt'.

Fernandez adapted quickly. In 1948, Dorothy and Cyril Burgess enrolled the young Fernandez at West Craven elementary school in Wombelton. It was here that he met Spanish teacher Phillipa Rose who would later become his life-long partner and interpreter.

In 1950, Fernandez was beginning to find the exciting new environment of Wakefield wearing a little thin. He was growing conscious of the harsh realities and low self esteem existing amongst the working classes. He began to draw inspiration from memories and experiences of his working life in Paraguay, and in 1953 invited 'Roberto Roena Y Su's Apollo Sound' to play a small working men's club in Timble. It proved highly popular and word soon began to spread.

It wasn't long before other clubs in the North began embracing this new latin thing; and it was infectious. The working classes were becoming exposed to a feel-good factor previously unknown to them. Within a week smiles were becoming frequent sights on the streets, from Skipton to Burnley and Huddersfield to Micklethwaite, and even Sheffield.

In 1959, riding high on the success of his popularity and the continued touring of 'Roberto Roena Y Su's Apollo Sound', Fernandez decided to put himself forward as a local council candidate in the upcoming Bubwith by-election. He won with a landslide majority, and cheers of 'Olé!' echoed around the town hall. In his famous four-hour election victory speech, interpreted by his now wife Phillipa, he pre-dated the modern political soundbite by 30 years. He punctuated with vernacular like 'Latin Music! Latin Music! Latin Music!', 'Tough on non-Latin Music! Tough on the causes of non-Latin Music!' and ended with the emphatic policy pledge: 'If music be the food of life, then you, the good people of Bubwith, shall have a huge slice of samba cake with a side order of calypso chips; and for the young and infirm, you will all get salsa buns!'.

With the jubilation of election night over, Fernandez now had to settle into his new role as councillor. He found himself in a position of power where he could now practice what he preached.

In 1962, Fernandez pushed through his first major policy towards social reform in the North. Inspired by the French radio policy that 80% of all music played should be French,

In his famous four-hour Bubwith by-election victory speech, Fernandez pre-dated the modern political soundbite by thirty years
Photo: Bubwith Council Archive

Fernandez made radio stations of the North play nothing but 100% Latin. It was an instant success. Productivity in the industrial area of Burnley rose by 68%; absenteeism in schools dropped by 78%.

These results confirmed what Fernandez had always truly believed: that Latin music, with regular exposure, can fill people with an overwhelming sense of happiness, and which in turn would bring about positive results for the whole community.

The following year he introduced Latin music on all public transport. The music of 'Orquesta Arangon' and 'Som Imaginrio' were for the first time being enjoyed by the people of Uppercumberworth. Marcus Selby writes, 'Juan

Pablo was riding the crest of a Mexican wave during his early years in governance. But a wave, like all waves, is made of water; and water, like all water, will eventually dry out or be collected in buckets'. In 1967, Fernandez' liquid-like popularity was beginning to get plumbing problems.

It was the 60s, and a new musical revolution was taking place outside the Latin Yorkshire borders. The Beatles were becoming the new sound and voice for the younger generation. The MLF (Musical Liberation Front) were gaining recognition and prominence in Kirby by illegally playing 'Hard Day's Night' and 'Help' using portable 4-track players as they knocked on people's doors canvassing for votes. Fearing an uprising, Fernandez decided to take desperate measures: Latin Musical Doorbells, Latin Musical Ice-Cream Vans, and emergency service sirens to a 6/8 beat. Those close to Fernandez were losing

faith and believed his vision for social change had now run out of Latin steam. Fernandez clung to power for the next two years only by relaxing some of his laws. He allowed the Beatles to be heard on radio stations for the first time, albeit overdubbed in Spanish. He was deposed in 1970 by Nigel Barnes.

Juan Pablo Fernandez' legacy and spirit lives on, though, and is still prevalent today in modern politics. Politicians and political parties are only too aware of the effect that choice music can have on society when played at certain times. When Tony Blair chose D-Ream's 'Things Can Only Get Better' for his 1997 general election campaign, he knew by that time tomorrow morning he'd be … well, the rest is history.

He is survived by his wife Phillipa and a son, Ringo.
Darren Buckingham

Juan Pablo Fernandez, politician & local councillor, born May 12th 1926; died August 6th 2004